Editor's Note

As this year's *Almanac* came together, several New York institutions were celebrating 100th anniversaries: WNYC (founded July 8, 1924), *The New Yorker* (February 21, 1925), NYPL's Schomburg Center (May 8, 1925), and the Morgan Library & Museum (March 28, 1924). I wondered: What does it take to make it more than 100 years in a city with a reputation for constant change? Tenacity? Attitude? Relevance? Funding?

The *Almanac* was created in 2022 to celebrate the city's tenacity as it recovered from the existential crisis of the COVID-19 pandemic. Today, many of the same organizations that helped New York through that dark time—some beloved for over a century—are facing a new crisis, as the federal government cancels funding they had relied on to carry out their missions.

Despite that threat, there is an astonishing variety of events, performances, and exhibitions already planned for the coming year. Please check with each institution, as dates are subject to change, and keep this edition handy as new events are announced.

July 4, 2026, marks another anniversary: the 250th anniversary of the US, a country founded on the ideals of equality and freedom. Let's celebrate those ideals not only by enjoying the inevitable fireworks and museum exhibitions about the American Revolution, but by supporting the city's cultural institutions—and the many points of view they represent—all year long.

The Five-Borough Fashion Forecast: All eyes are on the New York Stock Exchange as the nation remains in the grips of economic uncertainty. Will our wardrobes be as replete with recession indicators as the fashion soothsayers have foretold? Whether we regress to slender silhouettes reminiscent of wartime rationing remains to be seen, but signs generally point to subdued aesthetics in lieu of sartorial experimentation. You can count on fewer impulse purchases from frugal fashionistas, who will likely choose to invest in durable, versatile pieces over trendy slop. For the on-the-go New Yorker, there's no greater investment than a chic, reliable pair of walking shoes—especially in the age of congestion pricing, when Manhattanites may be more reluctant to hop in a cab or splurge on an Uber. Even as the MetroCard becomes a relic of the past, you can expect subway platforms to double as runways when stylish commuters take to the transit system.

The breakneck pace of the fashion cycle may finally slow down as tariffs threaten access to fast fashion brands produced overseas. American-made clothing will be at the center of the fashion conversation; perhaps the once-bustling Garment District could be headed for a renaissance. As microtrends driven by overconsumption start to dwindle, the growing secondhand market shows no signs of letting up—so look out for a boom on Depop and Poshmark, as well as at your local thrift store. The rising cost of clothing could drive customers to scratch that shopping itch with smaller, more attainable items, like beauty products and accessories. The craze for keychains and tchotchkes on handbags will stick around a while longer if the appetite for personalized kitsch persists.

As the wealth gap widens across the metropolis, we may well see the sartorial politics of the 1980s make a resurgence. Conspicuous consumption could mean the return of designer logos, luxurious fur, and gold hardware to Park Avenue. Meanwhile, urban professionals may return to power-dressing as they return to offices—armed with serious shoulder pads as they face down the competitive corporate landscape in FiDi and beyond.

Rest assured, New York City will remain a bastion of progressive ideals and the nation's undisputed fashion capital. Even in turbulent times, the city's bold and resilient style identity persists—so you can bet on New York fashion being as eclectic, vibrant, and of-the-moment as ever.

JANUARY

Since 1978, the city has bid farewell to the long holiday season with El Museo del Barrio's **Three Kings Day Parade**, stepping off at the frigid—sometimes snowy—intersection of 106th Street and Park Avenue in the heart of El Barrio (East Harlem). Giant puppets representing the Three Kings link the neighborhood's Puerto Rican culture with the island's traditional Taino heritage. At the end of the month—when the undertow of streaming-and-chill is the strongest—city boosters lure New Yorkers to get dressed and open their wallets for **Restaurant Week** (serving discounted prix-fixe menus at classy venues) and **Broadway Week** (offering two-for-one seats at hit shows). Catch **Jesse Malin at the Gramercy Theater**, find art and antiques at the **Winter Show** at the Park Avenue Armory, or bid on American-made treasures during **Americana Week** at Sotheby's and Christie's.

Outlook: *First week of the new year is bitter, but bright out . . . Then, during the second week, a winter storm could bring a whiteout. Maybe a half foot or more. Then dig out of your dungeon, for the mercury's plungin'. Very cold through the 19th, then a decided moderation as temperatures gradually rise. Thawsome!*

Normals for Central Park	
Average High: 39.5°	Thirty years ago, on January 6–7, 1996, the Tri-State area was hit by what is known in weather annals as the North American Blizzard of '96. The City University of New York reported that the storm "dropped 20 inches of snow [and] had wind gusts of 50 m.p.h. and snow drifts up to 8 feet high." Twenty years later, on January 22–23, 2016, Central Park saw its greatest single snowfall on record, at 27.5 inches.
Average Low: 27.9°	
Average Liquid Precipitation: 3.64"	
Average Snowfall: 8.8"	

Sky Watch: On January 3 at noon, Earth is at perihelion (closest to the Sun), at a distance of 91.4 million miles. But the Northern Hemisphere is at almost its farthest tilt away from the Sun, so our weather is cold. On the 4th, take note of the nearly full Moon positioned to the upper left of the brilliant planet Jupiter. On the 22nd, the slender sliver of a waxing crescent Moon is positioned well to the lower right of Saturn.

ANNALS OF THE NIGHT SKY

Forty years ago, on January 11, 1986, thousands of New Yorkers gathered at four city parks to get a view of Halley's Comet. Mayor Ed Koch and Parks Commissioner Henry J. Stern arranged to have the lights turned off at Prospect Park, Flushing Meadows-Corona Park, Rockaway Beach, and Van Cortlandt Park, where telescopes were set up. The comet itself was not overly impressive, but many were still happy to get a glimpse of it. As Stern put it: "Those who came for the comet saw the comet—the cynics didn't—but it was there."

NYC BOOK OF THE MONTH
The Best of Everything by Rona Jaffe (1958)

Jaffe sets the scene in chapter 1 on January 2, 1952, "one of those cold, foggy midwinter mornings in New York, the kind that makes you think of lung ailments." For research, Jaffe interviewed fifty women about their private lives, creating a frank, but still soapy, depiction of young working women in the mid-century city.

NYC MOVIE OF THE MONTH
Shadows, directed by John Cassavetes, starring Ben Carruthers, Lelia Goldoni, and Hugh Hurd (1959)

This independent film about Black jazz musician siblings, two of whom pass as white, was shot—without permits—at locations from Grand Central Terminal and the sculpture garden of the Museum of Modern Art to Cassavetes's own apartment. Despite some technical flaws, the realistic, improvised style sets the film apart as an arthouse classic.

Dec. 29–Jan. 4

"People talk about the death of New York ... when it turned out not to die, inconveniently for them, it was said to have lost its soul."
—Phillip Lopate

29 MONDAY
☼ 7:19 AM / 4:37 PM

The Magic Flute—Holiday Presentation at the Metropolitan Opera

30 TUESDAY
☼ 7:19 AM / 4:37 PM

Catch *Dress, Dreams, and Desire: Fashion and Psychoanalysis* at the Museum at FIT before it closes on Jan. 4

31 WEDNESDAY
☼ 7:19 AM / 4:38 PM

New Year's Eve

Bundle up for the New York Road Runners Midnight Run

1 THURSDAY
☼ 7:20 AM / 4:39 PM

New Year's Day
Kwanzaa ends.

Take the Polar Bear Plunge at Coney Island

2 FRIDAY
☼ 7:20 AM / 4:40 PM

Catch *Ministry: Reverend Joyce McDonald* at the Bronx Museum before it closes on Jan. 4

3 SATURDAY
☼ 7:20 AM / 4:41 PM ○ FULL MOON

Alvin Ailey American Dance Theater at New York City Center (through Jan. 4)

4 SUNDAY
☼ 7:20 AM / 4:42 PM

NYCRUNS Frozen Penguin 5K in Central Park

Jan. 5–11

"It must be the incredible towers and the lovely park and the rivers and the comings and goings of foreigners that raise false hopes in the hearts of even the most skeptical women and men."
—Kurt Vonnegut

5 MONDAY
☼ 7:20 AM / 4:43 PM

Metropolitan Opera presents *Porgy and Bess* (through Jan. 24)

6 TUESDAY
☼ 7:20 AM / 4:43 PM

Epiphany
Three Kings Day Parade, East Harlem

7 WEDNESDAY
☼ 7:20 AM / 4:44 PM

Orthodox Christmas Day
Winter Jazz Fest (through Jan. 13)

8 THURSDAY
☼ 7:19 AM / 4:45 PM

Catch *Marina Zurkow: Parting Worlds* at the Whitney Museum of American Art before it closes on Jan. 11

9 FRIDAY
☼ 7:19 AM / 4:46 PM

Third Annual Unity Jazz Festival at Jazz at Lincoln Center (and Jan. 10)

10 SATURDAY
☼ 7:19 AM / 4:48 PM   ☽ 3RD QUARTER

Metropolitan Opera presents a new production of *I Puritani* (through Jan. 18)

11 SUNDAY
☼ 7:19 AM / 4:49 PM

Jesse Malin plays Gramercy Theatre

Jan. 12–18

"New York is not a problem. New York is a stroke of genius."
—Ed Koch

12 MONDAY
☼ 7:18 AM / 4:50 PM

Catch *Sixties Surreal* at the Whitney Museum of American Art before it closes on Jan. 19

13 TUESDAY
☼ 7:18 AM / 4:51 PM

Metropolitan Opera presents *Madama Butterfly* (Jan. 9 through Mar. 28)

14 WEDNESDAY
☼ 7:18 AM / 4:52 PM

Orthodox New Year

NYCRUNS Frozen Pigeon 5K in Prospect Park, Brooklyn

15 THURSDAY
☼ 7:17 AM / 4:53 PM

Duke in Africa: the JLCO with Wynton Marsalis at Jazz at Lincoln Center (through Jan. 17)

16 FRIDAY
☼ 7:17 AM / 4:54 PM

Last chance to see *New Photography 2025: Lines of Belonging* at MoMA

17 SATURDAY
☼ 7:16 AM / 4:55 PM

Bi-2 Live plays Terminal 5

18 SUNDAY
☼ 7:16 AM / 4:56 PM ● NEW MOON

Last chance to see *Rashid Johnson: A Poem for Deep Thinkers* at the Guggenheim

Jan. 19–25

"Lower Manhattan has more real style in each crowded square foot than any other comparable city in the world.... The style...as everyone knows, is money."
—Ada Louise Huxtable

---

19 MONDAY

☼ 7:15 AM / 4:58 PM

Martin Luther King Jr. Day

Celebrate MLK Day at the Apollo Theater

---

20 TUESDAY

☼ 7:15 AM / 4:59 PM   ♒ AQUARIUS

Metropolitan Opera presents *Carmen* (through Jan. 23)

---

21 WEDNESDAY

☼ 7:14 AM / 5:00 PM

New York Boat Show at Javits Center (through Jan. 25)

---

22 THURSDAY

☼ 7:14 AM / 5:01 PM

New York City Ballet presents *Balanchine + Ratmansky* (and Jan. 20–21, 31, Feb. 1)

---

23 FRIDAY

☼ 7:13 AM / 5:02 PM

The Winter Show opens at the Park Avenue Armory (through Feb. 1)

---

24 SATURDAY

☼ 7:12 AM / 5:04 PM

New York City Ballet presents *Masters at Work II* (and Jan. 23, 25, 27–28)

---

25 SUNDAY

☼ 7:11 AM / 5:05 PM

Last chance to see *Shifting Landscapes* at the Whitney Museum of American Art

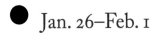

Jan. 26–Feb. 1

"New York is a city of things unnoticed."
—Gay Talese

26 MONDAY

☼ 7:11 AM / 5:06 PM   ☽ 1ST QUARTER

Catch *Man Ray: When Objects Dream* at the Metropolitan Museum of Art before it closes on Feb. 1

27 TUESDAY

☼ 7:10 AM / 5:07 PM

International Holocaust Remembrance Day

1895: Harry Ruby (Rubenstein), composer of "A Kiss to Build a Dream On," is born in New York City

28 WEDNESDAY

☼ 7:09 AM / 5:08 PM

1888: Jacob Riis presents his slide lecture "The Other Half: How It Lives and Dies in New York"

29 THURSDAY

☼ 7:08 AM / 5:10 PM

New York City Ballet presents *New Combinations* (and Jan. 30–31, Feb. 3–4, 7)

30 FRIDAY

☼ 7:07 AM / 5:11 PM

Come Sunday: The Sacred Works of Duke Ellington at Jazz at Lincoln Center (and Jan. 31)

31 SATURDAY

☼ 7:06 AM / 5:12 PM

150th Annual Westminster Kennel Club Dog Show at Javits Center and MSG (and Feb. 2–3)

1 SUNDAY

☼ 7:05 AM / 5:13 PM   ○ FULL MOON

Last chance to see *Monet and Venice* at the Brooklyn Museum

FEBRUARY

FORGET PARIS. FORGET ROME. *New York* is the most romantic city—so long as you're wearing just the right shade of rose-colored glasses. Smelly steam inexplicably gushing from an orange-and-white pipe in the middle of Lexington Avenue lends a misty glow to traffic in the evening light. Even in the depths of winter, the city is full of alluring strangers: the glamorous woman alone at a hotel bar, the owner of an outstretched hand helping you across a street-corner slush puddle, the chatty basketball fan on the train to Barclays Center. Yes, the subway can be romantic if you look past the, um, obvious—you don't even need Craigslist Missed Connections. On Valentine's Day, you might stumble on *Tunnel of Love*, artist Ruvan Wijesooriya's installation of thousands of free 4x6-inch love-themed prints. February is also your chance to see **Patti LuPone play Carnegie Hall**—and your last chance to see **NYPL's exhibition celebrating the *New Yorker*'s centennial.**

OUTLOOK: *As the month kicks off, no flummery . . . it almost feels summery! Perhaps accompanied by a rumble of thunder; even the groundhog is confused. Unfortunately, by the holiday weekend, it's back to normality . . . a rain/snow reality. Folks living north and west of NYC might see up to a foot of the white stuff. As we approach month's end, it's mush and slush, by gush!*

NORMALS FOR CENTRAL PARK	
Average High: 42.2°	Fifty years ago, on February 2, 1976, most self-respecting groundhogs were looking for their fur coats and not their shadows. NYC experienced a flash freeze, with temperatures dropping sharply from the 40s at 4 a.m. to 17° at 7 a.m. Half an inch of rain fell before changing to snow, which accumulated to 1" at Central Park by 8 a.m. Rain-soaked pavements turned icy with gusty winds up to 50 m.p.h. Area airports shut down during the morning.
Average Low: 29.5°	
Average Liquid Precipitation: 3.19"	
Average Snowfall: 10.1"	

Sky Watch: On the 2nd, bluish Regulus—one of the twenty-one brightest stars, and the brightest in the constellation of Leo—will be hidden (occulted) by a waxing gibbous Moon between 8:53 p.m. and 9:52 p.m. On the 18th, forty-five minutes after sunset, look near the west-southwest horizon for a narrow crescent Moon. Directly above it, you'll see a very bright "star," which is really the nearest planet to the Sun, Mercury.

ANNALS OF THE NIGHT SKY

The farthest celestial object visible without a telescope is the Andromeda Galaxy, appearing as a faint elongated patch to the naked eye. Its light traveled for 2.5 million years to reach us, at a velocity of nearly 671 million miles per hour. When it began its 15-quintillion-mile journey earthward, mastodons and saber-toothed tigers roamed North America, and prehistoric man struggled for existence in what is now the Olduvai Gorge of East Africa. It is estimated that one trillion stars make up Andromeda, more than twice the number in our own Milky Way galaxy.

NYC BOOK OF THE MONTH
Lunch Poems by Frank O'Hara (1964)

O'Hara once told a Staten Island audience that he'd composed the poem "Lana Turner has collapsed!" while crossing from Manhattan on the ferry. The story goes that he wrote *Lunch Poems*—which embeds meaning in glimpses of the mundane cityscape—during his lunch breaks while working the admissions desk at the Museum of Modern Art, where he was later curator.

NYC MOVIE OF THE MONTH
The Thomas Crown Affair, directed by John McTiernan, starring Pierce Brosnan, Rene Russo, and Denis Leary (1999)

The singular focus of Thomas Crown, sitting on the same bench, eyeing the same painting every day, is the kind of attention museum curators dream of—less so his theft of a Monet, which sets this romance/heist film in motion. The Met declined filming inside its galleries, but its exterior, along with glitzy spots like the Sherry Netherland Hotel, appears onscreen.

Feb. 2–8

"If you grew up anywhere in the city, there is a good chance your childhood memories will be bundled with tangible goods and sold to the highest bidder before you reach adulthood."
—Sasha Frere-Jones

2 MONDAY
☼ 7:04 AM / 5:15 PM

Groundhog Day

Carnegie Hall presents Patti LuPone

3 TUESDAY
☼ 7:03 AM / 5:16 PM

Catch *Renoir Drawings* at the Morgan Library and Museum before it closes on Feb. 8

4 WEDNESDAY
☼ 7:02 AM / 5:17 PM

Frank Vignola's Guitar Night at Birdland jazz club (Wednesdays)

5 THURSDAY
☼ 7:01 AM / 5:18 PM

New York City Ballet presents *Contemporary Choreography II* (and Feb. 6–8, 24, 25)

6 FRIDAY
☼ 7:00 AM / 5:19 PM

Carnegie Hall presents the Budapest Festival Orchestra

7 SATURDAY
☼ 6:59 AM / 5:21 PM

Last chance to see *Ruth Asawa: A Retrospective* at MoMA

8 SUNDAY
☼ 6:58 AM / 5:22 PM

Last chance to see *Witnessing Humanity: The Art of John Wilson* at the Metropolitan Museum of Art

Feb. 9–15

"It was really snowing and / raining and I was in such a hurry / to meet you but the traffic / was acting exactly like the sky."
—Frank O'Hara

---

9 MONDAY

☼ 6:57 AM / 5:23 PM ◑ 3RD QUARTER

1969: A fifteen-inch blizzard paralyzes the city, nearly ending Mayor Lindsay's political career

---

10 TUESDAY

☼ 6:56 AM / 5:24 PM

1956: Muralist and artist Manny Vega is born in the Bronx

---

11 WEDNESDAY

☼ 6:54 AM / 5:26 PM

New York City Ballet presents *The Sleeping Beauty* (and Feb. 12–15, 17–22)

---

12 THURSDAY

☼ 6:53 AM / 5:27 PM

Lincoln's Birthday

Catch *An Ecology of Quilts: The Natural History of American Textiles* at the American Folk Art Museum before it closes on Mar. 1

---

13 FRIDAY

☼ 6:52 AM / 5:28 PM

Dianne Reeves at Jazz at Lincoln Center (and Feb. 14)

---

14 SATURDAY

☼ 6:51 AM / 5:29 PM

Valentine's Day

NYCRUNS Frozen Bonsai 5K in Prospect Park, Brooklyn

---

15 SUNDAY

☼ 6:49 AM / 5:30 PM

Susan B. Anthony's Birthday

Last chance to see *Colorful Korea: The Lea R. Sneider Collection* at the Metropolitan Museum of Art

Feb. 16–22

"Most people accept New York's mayhem as some kind of toll, a small price to pay for the panoply of delights available to them at a moment's notice."
—Lena Dunham

16 MONDAY
☼ 6:48 AM / 5:32 PM

Presidents' Day

Kids Week at the Intrepid Museum (Feb. 14–21)

17 TUESDAY
☼ 6:47 AM / 5:33 PM ● NEW MOON

Lunar New Year
Ramadan begins.

Catch *Blazing a Trail: Dorothy Waugh's National Parks Posters* at the Poster House before it closes on Feb. 22

18 WEDNESDAY
☼ 6:45 AM / 5:34 PM ♓ PISCES

Ash Wednesday

Catch *Breaking the Mold: Brooklyn Museum at 200* at the Brooklyn Museum before it closes on Feb. 22

19 THURSDAY
☼ 6:44 AM / 5:35 PM

Lyon Opera Ballet at New York City Center (through Feb. 21)

20 FRIDAY
☼ 6:43 AM / 5:36 PM

Arnhold Innovation Series: Jeremy Pelt and Endea Owens at Jazz at Lincoln Center (and Feb. 21)

21 SATURDAY
☼ 6:41 AM / 5:38 PM

Last chance to see *A Century of The New Yorker* at NYPL's Schwarzman Building

22 SUNDAY
☼ 6:40 AM / 5:39 PM

Last chance to see *Urban Stomp* at the Museum of the City of New York

Feb. 23–Mar. 1

"Times Square about six o'clock... Broadway's finest hour. Here, until midnight, New York takes its bath of light."
—Paul Morand, 1930

23 MONDAY
☼ 6:38 AM / 5:40 PM

1940: Peter Fonda is born in New York

24 TUESDAY
☼ 6:37 AM / 5:41 PM ☽ 1ST QUARTER

1931: Actor Dominic Chianese ("Uncle Junior" in *The Sopranos*) is born in the Bronx

25 WEDNESDAY
☼ 6:35 AM / 5:42 PM

New York Philharmonic's Lunar New Year Gala

26 THURSDAY
☼ 6:34 AM / 5:43 PM

25th Flamenco Festival at New York City Center (through Mar. 8)

27 FRIDAY
☼ 6:32 AM / 5:45 PM

Arnhold Innovation Series: Carlos Henriquez and Obed Calvaire at Jazz at Lincoln Center

28 SATURDAY
☼ 6:31 AM / 5:46 PM

MANÁ Vivir Sin Aire Tour at Barclays Center

1 SUNDAY
☼ 6:29 AM / 5:47 PM

New York City Ballet presents *Masters at Work II* (and Feb. 26–28)

MARCH

THERE ARE TWO GOOD REASONS TO BELLY UP to the bar for an ale (light or dark only) at McSorley's Old Ale House in March. The first is **St. Patrick's Day**: Irish immigrant John McSorley opened the city's oldest continually operating saloon in 1854, and its owners have been connected to Ireland ever since. The second is **Women's History Month**. In 1970, Faith Seidenberg and Karen DeCrow sued the establishment for its male-only policy. That August 10, the same day Mayor Lindsay signed a law prohibiting discrimination in public places on the basis of sex, the bar's manager escorted friend and neighbor Barbara Shaum through its storied doors. For a less traditional take on St. Patrick's Day, the **St. Pat's for All Parade**—founded in 2000 in response to the exclusion of LGBTQ+ marchers from Fifth Avenue's parade—kicks off in the Sunnyside and Woodside neighborhoods of Queens. Or learn about the life of a mid-nineteenth-century Irish servant at **Merchant's House Museum**.

OUTLOOK: *Does the month kick off like a lion or lamb? Here's a clue: Batten down your hatches—a nor'easter brings batches! From the 12th through the 15th, there's no risk in saying it's brisk. And for good measure, let's also mention some showers of rain and wet snow. During March's third week, great days for the Irish and all their friends. Seems like spring's dress rehearsal, but by month's end—drat! A reversal.*

NORMALS FOR CENTRAL PARK	
Average High: 49.9°	What some might call a "double whammy" snowfall took place during the March 16–18 timeframe in 1956. The first storm, on the 16th, deposited 4.6", which had melted down to a "slip cover" of ½" of ice when the second storm roared in on the 18th. Local forecasts called only for flurries, but in the end, 13.5" accumulated at Central Park and many travelers became stranded.
Average Low: 35.8°	
Average Liquid Precipitation: 4.29"	
Average Snowfall: 5.0"	

Sky Watch: During the early hours of Tuesday, March 3, the Moon will undergo a total eclipse. But for New Yorkers, this event will occur under special circumstances. When the Moon begins to enter the Earth's dark shadow at 4:49 a.m., it will already be rather low in the western sky. At totality at 6:03 a.m., the Moon will be barely above the horizon, and it will set twenty-five minutes later still in total eclipse.

ANNALS OF THE NIGHT SKY

Contrary to popular belief, Galileo Galilei did not invent the telescope. It was a Dutch spectacle-maker, Hans Lippershey, who first applied for a telescope patent in 1608. Apparently, the device was originally used as a spyglass to observe sailing ships so distant that they were two hours or more from being visible to the unaided eye. But a year later, in 1609, Galileo became the first person to use a telescope to view the Sun, Moon, and planets.

NYC BOOK OF THE MONTH
St. Marks Is Dead: The Many Lives of America's Hippest Street
by Ada Calhoun (2015)

Calhoun takes a long view of the history of a fairly short block in this nonfiction chronicle of St. Mark's Place. The rare child who actually grew up on St. Mark's, she interviewed hundreds of current and former residents, tracing how the denizens of each era decried the street's inevitable death—only to find it born again into a new era.

NYC MOVIE OF THE MONTH
Big, directed by Penny Marshall, starring Tom Hanks, Elizabeth Perkins, Robert Loggia, and John Heard (1988)

Hanks's performance as a gobsmacked, guileless thirteen-year-old who accidentally, magically, turns into an adult and winds up vice president of a toy company makes an absurd plot charming. The film features a classic piece of New York movie-making when Hanks and his boss play "Heart and Soul" on the "walking" piano at FAO Schwartz on Fifth Ave.

Mar. 2–8

"Each generation is drawn by a collective memory of New York and the miracle of regeneration."
—Ada Louise Huxtable

---

2 MONDAY

☼ 6:28 AM / 5:48 PM ○ FULL MOON

Carnegie Hall presents *The Secret Life of the American Musical*

---

3 TUESDAY

☼ 6:26 AM / 5:49 PM

Purim

1943: Lucille Armstrong puts a down payment on the Corona, Queens, house (now a museum) that she will share with Louis Armstrong until 1971

---

4 WEDNESDAY

☼ 6:25 AM / 5:50 PM

New York International Children's Film Festival (Feb. 27–Mar. 15)

---

5 THURSDAY

☼ 6:23 AM / 5:51 PM

Catch *Emily Sargent: Portrait of a Family* at the Metropolitan Museum of Art before it closes on Mar. 9

---

6 FRIDAY

☼ 6:22 AM / 5:52 PM

Big Band Afrobeat: Ulysses Owens Jr. and Michael Olatuja at Jazz at Lincoln Center (and Mar. 7)

---

7 SATURDAY

☼ 6:20 AM / 5:54 PM

Family Concert: Who Is Louis Armstrong? at Jazz at Lincoln Center

---

8 SUNDAY

☼ 7:18 AM / 6:55 PM

International Women's Day
Daylight saving time begins.

Last chance to see *The Gay Harlem Renaissance* at the New York Historical

# Mar. 9–15

"This great, plunging, dramatic, ferocious, swift, and terrible city is the most provincial place I have lived in."
—Alistair Cooke

9 MONDAY
☼ 7:17 AM / 6:56 PM

The Metropolitan Opera presents a new production of *Tristan und Isolde* (through Apr. 2)

10 TUESDAY
☼ 7:15 AM / 6:57 PM

Carnegie Hall presents the Philadelphia Orchestra

11 WEDNESDAY
☼ 7:14 AM / 6:58 PM   ☽ 3RD QUARTER

2026 New York Wind Band Festival at Carnegie Hall

12 THURSDAY
☼ 7:12 AM / 6:59 PM

1987: Larry Kramer and others found AIDS Coalition to Unleash Power (ACT UP) at the Lesbian and Gay Community Services Center

13 FRIDAY
☼ 7:10 AM / 7:00 PM

Arnhold Innovation Series: Danilo Perez and Godwin Louis at Jazz at Lincoln Center (and Mar. 12, 14)

14 SATURDAY
☼ 7:09 AM / 7:01 PM

Gustavo Dudamel conducts *Eroica* & *The People United Will Never Be Defeated* at the New York Philharmonic

15 SUNDAY
☼ 7:07 AM / 7:02 PM

Lailat al-Qadr

"In the Footsteps of Bridget Murphy: The Life of an Irish Servant" tour at Merchant's House Museum

Mar. 16–22

"Elaine's, the place to drink and eat: / The crowd's elite, and so's the meat. / Elaine herself, 'tis sad to say, / Tells common people, 'Go away.'"
  —Alan Rich, 1977

16 MONDAY

☼ 7:05 AM / 7:03 PM

Last chance to see *Ayoung Kim* at MoMA PS1

17 TUESDAY

☼ 7:04 AM / 7:04 PM

Saint Patrick's Day

Stone Street St. Paddy's Day Street Fest (featuring "Shamrock Margaritas")

18 WEDNESDAY

☼ 7:02 AM / 7:06 PM ● NEW MOON

Ramadan ends.

Catch *Seeing Silence: The Paintings of Helene Schjerfbeck* at the Metropolitan Museum of Art before it closes on Apr. 5

19 THURSDAY

☼ 7:00 AM / 7:07 PM

Gustavo Dudamel conducts *the wealth of nations* at New York Philharmonic

20 FRIDAY

6:59 AM / 7:08 PM ♈ ARIES

Vernal Equinox
Eid al-Fitr

Metropolitan Opera presents *La Traviata* (through Jun. 6)

21 SATURDAY

☼ 6:57 AM / 7:09 PM

Michael Feinstein's Tribute to Tony Bennett at Kupferberg Center for the Arts, Queens

22 SUNDAY

☼ 6:56 AM / 7:10 PM

Last chance to see *Robert Rauschenberg's New York: Pictures from the Real World* at the Museum of the City of New York

Mar. 23–29

"The illusion that the city gives, to almost anybody, [is] that he must be accomplishing something by talking or eating or drinking or reading a newspaper in such a busy, expensive place."
—Kurt Vonnegut

23 MONDAY
☼ 6:54 AM / 7:11 PM

1857: Otis installs the first steam-powered hydraulic elevator in the E. V. Haughwout & Co. department store on Broome St. and Broadway

24 TUESDAY
☼ 6:52 AM / 7:12 PM ☽ 1ST QUARTER

Artist Spotlight: Sheku & Isata Kanneh-Mason at New York Philharmonic

25 WEDNESDAY
☼ 6:51 AM / 7:13 PM

Catch *Heaven & Earth: The Blue Maps of China* at Museum of Chinese in America before it closes on Mar. 29

26 THURSDAY
☼ 6:59 AM / 7:14 PM

New York City Center Encores! presents *The Wild Party* (Mar. 18–29)

27 FRIDAY
☼ 6:47 AM / 7:15 PM

Bill Frisell: 75th Birthday Celebration at Jazz at Lincoln Center

28 SATURDAY
☼ 6:56 AM / 7:16 PM

Last chance to see *Searching for Superpublics* and *Making Energy Visible* at the Center for Architecture

29 SUNDAY
☼ 6:44 AM / 7:17 PM

Palm Sunday

Last chance to see *Arriving in America: Portraits of Immigrants from the New York Historical Collections* at the New York Historical

Mar. 30–Apr. 5

"Dawn in New York has / four columns of mire / and a hurricane of black pigeons / splashing in the putrid waters."
  —Federico García Lorca, translated by Greg Simon and Steven L. White

30 MONDAY

☼ 6:42 AM / 7:18 PM

Catch *The Socrates Annual 2025* at Socrates Sculpture Park, Queens, before it closes on Apr. 6

31 TUESDAY

☼ 6:41 AM / 7:19 PM

Celebrate Transgender Day of Visibility at the Lesbian, Gay, Bisexual & Transgender Community Center

1 WEDNESDAY

☼ 6:39 AM / 7:20 PM

April Fool's Day
Passover begins.

Last chance to see *The Jousting Armor of Philip I of Castile* at the Metropolitan Museum of Art

2 THURSDAY

☼ 6:37 AM / 7:21 PM
○ FULL MOON

New York City Public Schools Spring Recess begins (through Apr. 10)

3 FRIDAY

☼ 6:36 AM / 7:22 PM

Good Friday

New York International Auto Show at Javits Center (through Apr. 12)

4 SATURDAY

☼ 6:34 AM / 7:23 PM

Last chance to see *Ideas of Africa: Portraiture and Political Imagination* at MoMA

5 SUNDAY

☼ 6:32 AM / 7:25 PM

Easter Sunday

Easter Parade on Fifth Avenue in front of St. Patrick's Cathedral

APRIL

WASHINGTON, D.C., MIGHT *think* it owns **cherry blossom season**, but New Yorkers can find thousands of blossoming cherry trees throughout the five boroughs. Every New Yorker has a favorite cherry tree. Maybe it's one of the more than 200 at the Brooklyn Botanic Garden, or one of the 6,800 in city parks. Or maybe it's one of the more than 38,000 Japanese flowering cherry trees that dot the city streets—the perfect one just outside the window of a Brooklyn brownstone, the scrappy one defiantly blooming on a busy midtown block, or the lush one providing just the right amount of shade to your favorite restaurant's outdoor tables. Visit the West Side Community Garden (West 89th Street) during their **Tulip Festival** to see more than 10,000 bulbs bloom; celebrate **Record Store Day** at Rockefeller Center's Rough Trade, Greenwich Village's Generation Records, or Carroll Gardens' Black Gold (where you can get coffee and antiques, too); and take in the **Print Fair** at the Park Avenue Armory.

OUTLOOK: *Our Easter Forecast is for occasional flowers, followed by skies clearing "rabbit-ly." From the 7th through the 12th, look for April showers (they bring May doubleheaders). Then a return to sun and warmer weather just about the same time the IRS takes the shirt off your back. The last ten days of April are perfect for biking or hiking; just watch out toward month's end for lightning striking!*

NORMALS FOR CENTRAL PARK	
Average High: 61.8°	April 18, 1976, was Easter Sunday, made especially memorable by temperatures more apropos for midsummer. The thermometer hit 96°, breaking the old record for April 18: 90°, set in 1896. It was also the hottest Easter on record, easily surpassing the old record of 86°, set twice on April 22 in 1962 and 1973. And for the only time in history, NYC had the highest temperature in the nation!
Average Low: 45.5°	
Average Liquid Precipitation: 4.09"	
Average Snowfall: 0.4"	

Sky Watch: On April 18, an hour after sunset, look low to the west-northwest to see dazzling Venus hovering well to the left of a hairline-thin crescent Moon. On the following evening, the Moon's position will have shifted to the upper left of the beautiful Pleiades star cluster. On the 22nd, a nearly half Moon sits to the upper right of Jupiter, with the "Twin Stars," Pollux and Castor, hovering directly above.

ANNALS OF THE NIGHT SKY

How many stars shine bright enough for us to see with our eyes alone, in places where there is no light pollution? The Yale Bright Star Catalogue provides the answer: 9,095. Of course, we could never see all of them at once, since at least half would fall below the horizon. There's also the problem of haze, which severely reduces the number of stars visible near the horizon, even under ideal skies. Due to these factors, the total number of stars we can see at night at any given moment is around 2,500.

NYC BOOK OF THE MONTH
Bodega: Poems by Su Hwang (2019)

Hwang's poems explore the tensions surrounding the immigrant experience in New York, through the perspective of a Korean girl coming of age in her parents' bodega in the Queensbridge housing projects. The poems shift from verse to blocks of prose, while the city itself comes alive not just as a backdrop but as a true habitat that shapes its residents.

NYC MOVIE OF THE MONTH

It Should Happen to You, directed by George Cukor, starring Judy Holliday, Peter Lawford, and Jack Lemmon (1954)

One of Martin Scorsese's favorite movies, this satire about the quest for, and meaning of, fame—which Holliday's Gladys achieves by posting her name on billboards all over town—was filmed on location. It includes beautiful footage of Central Park at mid-century.

Apr. 6–12

"Take Harlem's heartbeat, /
Make a drumbeat, / Put it on a
record, let it whirl, / And while
we listen to it play, / Dance with
you till day..."
 —Langston Hughes

---

6 MONDAY

☼ 6:31 AM / 7:26 PM

The Metropolitan Opera presents a new production of *Innocence* (Apr. 6–29)

---

7 TUESDAY

☼ 6:29 AM / 7:27 PM

1818: Brooks Brothers is founded

---

8 WEDNESDAY

☼ 6:28 AM / 7:28 PM

Catch *Christian Marclay: Doors* at the Brooklyn Museum before it closes on Apr. 12

---

9 THURSDAY

☼ 6:26 AM / 7:29 PM

Passover ends.

Martha Graham Dance Company celebrates their centennial at New York City Center (through Apr. 12)

---

10 FRIDAY

☼ 6:24 AM / 7:30 PM   ☽ 3RD QUARTER

The IFPDA Print Fair opens at the Park Avenue Armory (through Apr. 12)

---

11 SATURDAY

☼ 6:23 AM / 7:31 PM

Journey Through Jazz: Overtures to Africa at Jazz at Lincoln Center (and Apr. 10)

---

12 SUNDAY

☼ 6:21 AM / 7:32 PM

Orthodox Easter Sunday

Last chance to see *Utopia in Our Time: The Posters of Molly Crabapple* at Poster House

Apr. 13–19

"Upon the clothes behind the tenement, / That hang like ghosts suspended from the lines, / Linking each flat, but to each indifferent, / Incongruous and strange the moonlight shines."
—Claude McKay

---

13 MONDAY

☼ 6:20 AM / 7:33 PM

1870: The Metropolitan Museum of Art is incorporated

---

14 TUESDAY

☼ 6:18 AM / 7:34 PM

Mets and Yankees celebrate Jackie Robinson Day by wearing number 42

---

15 WEDNESDAY

☼ 6:17 AM / 7:35 PM

Tax Day

Jazz Jam with Ray Scro at Superfine in DUMBO (second and fourth Wednesdays, monthly)

---

16 THURSDAY

☼ 6:15 AM / 7:36 PM

Dance Theatre of Harlem at New York City Center (through Apr. 19)

---

17 FRIDAY

☼ 6:14 AM / 7:37 PM   ● NEW MOON

Birth of the Blues: The JLCO with Wynton Marsalis at Jazz at Lincoln Center (and Apr. 18)

---

18 SATURDAY

☼ 6:12 AM / 7:38 PM

Celebrate Record Store Day with Rough Trade at Rockefeller Center

---

19 SUNDAY

☼ 6:11 AM / 7:39 PM

Catch *Gabriele Münter: Into Deep Waters* at the Guggenheim before it closes on Apr. 26

Apr. 20–26

"I want to fall asleep on my own fire escape / and wake up dazed and hungry / to the sound of garbage grinding in the street below / and the smell of coffee cooking in the window above."
—Gerald Stern

---

20 MONDAY

☼ 6:09 AM / 7:40 PM ♉ TAURUS

1939: Billie Holiday records "Strange Fruit" with members of New York's Café Society band

---

21 TUESDAY

☼ 6:08 AM / 7:41 PM

New York City Ballet presents *All Balanchine*, including *Firebird* (and Apr. 24–25, 30, May 2–3)

---

22 WEDNESDAY

☼ 6:06 AM / 7:42 PM

Earth Day

Celebrate Earth Day with a day of service in a city park

---

23 THURSDAY

☼ 6:05 AM / 7:43 PM

Calum Scott plays Terminal 5

---

24 FRIDAY

☼ 6:04 AM / 7:44 PM ☽ 1ST QUARTER

Arbor Day

Ballet Hispánico at New York City Center (Apr. 23–26)

---

25 SATURDAY

☼ 6:02 AM / 7:45 PM

Ski Aggu plays Webster Hall

---

26 SUNDAY

☼ 6:01 AM / 7:47 PM

NYCRUNS Brooklyn Experience Half Marathon

Apr. 27–May 3

"April in Paris has nothing on May in New York. Spring happens to the city as everything happens here: not at all, then all at once."
—Alexandra Schwartz

---

27 MONDAY
☼ 5:59 AM / 7:48 PM

Catch *German Masterworks from the Neue Galerie* at the Neue Galerie before it closes May 4

---

28 TUESDAY
☼ 5:58 AM / 7:49 PM

Carnegie Hall Presents Lisa Batiashvili, violin, and Giorgi Gigashvili, piano

---

29 WEDNESDAY
☼ 5:57 AM / 7:50 PM

Celebrate Poem in Your Pocket Day with verses from Bronx-born poet Roya Marsh

---

30 THURSDAY
☼ 5:55 AM / 7:51 PM

66th Annual ABAA New York International Antiquarian Book Fair (through May 3)

---

1 FRIDAY
☼ 5:54 AM / 7:52 PM   ○ FULL MOON

Vesak

The Occupied City: New York and the American Revolution opens at the Museum of the City of New York

---

2 SATURDAY
☼ 5:53 AM / 7:53 PM

Don your hats, sip your mint juleps, and head to Brooklyn Derby for a Kentucky Derby watch party

---

3 SUNDAY
☼ 5:52 AM / 7:54 PM

TD Five Boro Bike Tour

MAY

MAY KICKS OFF WITH GLAMOROUS starlets, fashion designers, and what's left of the magazine industry **partying in support of the Metropolitan Museum of Art's Costume Institute**. It ends with the official start of summer: Memorial Day. In between, celebrate AAPI month at the **Asian Comedy Festival**, or dress as your best approximation of a southern dandy for one of the city's many Kentucky Derby watch parties—like **Brooklyn Derby**, started by a Kentucky native and his roommates. If you're feeling hungry, head to the **Bronx Night Market** for local food-truck delicacies; if you're feeling sporty, pedal through car-free streets for the **Five Boro Bike Tour**. Or grab a paddle and head to **Wolman Rink in Central Park** to play the nation's fastest-growing sport—pickleball—if your dignity can stand it.

OUTLOOK: *May's first week boasts pleasant temperatures and clear blue skies; it's azure thing! A brief interlude from fair weather between the 8th and 11th, as stormy conditions offer an "enlightning" experience. Then back to another week of fair skies. Spring now seems springier, but alas, too good to linger. We'll close out the month on a wet note, cool and pouring; by Memorial Day, it'll be getting boring.*

NORMALS FOR
CENTRAL PARK
Average High: 71.4°
Average Low: 55.0°
Average Liquid
Precipitation: 3.96"

| May is the month of new green. Within the span of a few weeks, sometimes even less, a bleak gray-brown landscape turns into a riot of shades of green, from yellowish to bluish. The local flowers of May—dogwoods, lilacs, and later rhododendrons—add accent colors to the basic theme of rapidly unfolding green. The normal high temperature jumps from 58° in April to 71° in May.

SKY WATCH: About an hour after sunset on May 18, check out a striking celestial tableau low in the west-northwest sky as a two-day-old crescent Moon snuggles close to Venus. On the evening of the 20th, a somewhat wider lunar crescent is positioned well to the upper left of Jupiter. During the final week of May, watch how Venus approaches Jupiter, building toward an eye-catching rendezvous on June 9.

ANNALS OF THE NIGHT SKY

Astronomy is the oldest of the sciences. Therefore, amateur astronomy can rightfully claim to be the oldest of the scientific hobbies. One such hobbyist, Garrett P. Serviss, earned a law degree at Columbia University but never became an attorney. Instead, he joined *The New York Sun* in 1878 and later became a renowned popularizer of astronomy. In 1910, he wrote: "Everybody may not be a chemist, a geologist, or a mathematician, but everybody may be, in a modest personal way, an astronomer, for star gazing is a great medicine of the soul."

NYC BOOK OF THE MONTH
The Custom of the Country by Edith Wharton (1913)

Perhaps the most modern of Wharton's novels—Jonathan Franzen called it "the first fictional rendering of a culture to which the Kardashians, Twitter, and Fox News would come as no surprise"—*The Custom of the Country* follows Undine Spragg, an unabashedly selfish "new money" beauty who takes social climbing to new heights as she gets the better of "Old New York" society.

NYC MOVIE OF THE MONTH
Fame, directed by Alan Parker, starring Eddie Barth, Irene Cara, Lee Curreri, Laura Dean, and others (1980)

Inspired by the musical *A Chorus Line*, *Fame* chronicles the lives of students at Manhattan's High School of Performing Arts. Although the city's Board of Ed. prevented the filming of actual classes, location filming started in July 1979, when students were not in school. Several students and teachers landed starring roles. The "Fame" musical number was shot on 46th Street with 150 students and 50 professional dancers.

May 4–10

"I saw Brooklyn differently from people who came there from Wisconsin or wherever. Behind every cute organic food store, I saw the ghost of the sad, dark, odiferous grocerette of my childhood."
—Roz Chast

4 MONDAY
☼ 5:50 AM / 7:55 PM

The Metropolitan Museum of Art's Costume Institute Gala

5 TUESDAY
☼ 5:49 AM / 7:56 PM

Cinco de Mayo

Carnegie Hall presents *50th Anniversary of the Concert of the Century*, a celebration of a legendary event in Carnegie Hall's history

6 WEDNESDAY
☼ 5:48 AM / 7:57 PM

1926: The New York Public Library acquires Arturo Schomburg's collection, the foundation of the Schomburg Center for Research in Black Culture

7 THURSDAY
☼ 5:47 AM / 7:58 PM

Gustavo Dudamel conducts the Spanish Harlem Orchestra at New York Philharmonic

8 FRIDAY
☼ 5:46 AM / 7:59 PM

Carnegie Hall presents Rhiannon Giddens

9 SATURDAY
☼ 5:45 AM / 8:00 PM   ☽ 3RD QUARTER

Oscar Peterson: A Centennial Celebration at Jazz at Lincoln Center (and May 8)

10 SUNDAY
☼ 5:43 AM / 8:01 PM

Mother's Day

Mother's Day Tour at Merchant's House Museum

May 11–17

"As usual in New York, everything is torn down / Before you have had time to care for it."
—Frank O'Hara

11 MONDAY
☼ 5:42 AM / 8:02 PM

The American Art Fair at Bohemian National Hall (May 9–12)

12 TUESDAY
☼ 5:41 AM / 8:03 PM

The Metropolitan Opera presents *Eugene Onegin* (Apr. 20–May 16)

13 WEDNESDAY
☼ 5:40 AM / 8:04 PM

1911: The Brooklyn Botanic Garden opens

14 THURSDAY
☼ 5:39 AM / 8:04 PM

Ascension Day

Sketches of Miles: Miles Davis at 100 at Jazz at Lincoln Center (and May 15–16)

15 FRIDAY
☼ 5:38 AM / 8:06 PM

Bike to Work Day—with support from Transportation Alternatives and NYCDOT

16 SATURDAY
☼ 5:38 AM / 8:07 PM ● NEW MOON

Artist Spotlight: Samara Joy at New York Philharmonic

17 SUNDAY
☼ 5:37 AM / 8:08 PM

New York City Ballet presents a sensory-friendly performance

May 18–24

"There is little in New York that does not issue out of money... but what issues out of money is often extremely brilliant."
—H. L. Mencken

18 MONDAY
☼ 5:36 AM / 8:09 PM

Carnegie Hall presents the Met Orchestra Chamber Ensemble

19 TUESDAY
☼ 5:35 AM / 8:10 PM

1941: Nora Ephron is born in New York

20 WEDNESDAY
☼ 5:34 AM / 8:11 PM   ♊ GEMINI

1972: Busta Rhymes (Trevor George Smith Jr.) is born in East Flatbush, Brooklyn

21 THURSDAY
☼ 5:33 AM / 8:12 PM

Shavuot begins.

New York City Ballet presents *All Bach* (May 13, 15–16, 21)

22 FRIDAY
☼ 5:33 AM / 8:12 PM

Sound On: Nathalie Joachim at New York Philharmonic

23 SATURDAY
☼ 5:32 AM / 8:13 PM   ◐ 1ST QUARTER

Shavuot ends.

New York City Ballet presents *Coppélia* (and May 22, 24, 29–31)

24 SUNDAY
☼ 5:31 AM / 8:14 PM

Loisaida Festival on the Lower East Side

May 25–31

"The fire escape, poised delicately between the precariousness of domestic life and the dangers of the world outside, is where stories begin."
— Shahnaz Habib

---

25 MONDAY
☼ 5:30 AM / 8:15 PM

Memorial Day

Memorial Day Ceremony at the Intrepid Museum

---

26 TUESDAY
☼ 5:30 AM / 8:16 PM

The Metropolitan Opera presents a new production of *El Último Sueño de Frida y Diego* (May 14–Jun. 5)

---

27 WEDNESDAY
☼ 5:29 AM / 8:17 PM

Eid al-Adha

Carnegie Hall presents Maxim Vengerov, violin, and Polina Osetinskaya, piano

---

28 THURSDAY
☼ 5:29 AM / 8:18 PM

Sheku Kanneh-Mason Plays Elgar, New York Philharmonic (May 27–30)

---

29 FRIDAY
☼ 5:28 AM / 8:18 PM

South Bronx Cultural Festival (through May 31)

---

30 SATURDAY
☼ 5:28 AM / 8:19 PM

Jazzmeia Horn and Her Noble Force at Jazz at Lincoln Center (and May 29)

---

31 SUNDAY
☼ 5:27 AM / 8:20 PM   ○ FULL MOON

Last chance to see *Iba Ndiaye: Between Latitude and Longitude* at the Metropolitan Museum of Art

JUNE

THE TOMATOES MAY BE REDOLENT of car exhaust, the lettuce leaves sprinkled with oily black dust, the strawberries nipped by a passing rat or inquisitive squirrel, and the entire enterprise of questionable legality—but intrepid fire-escape gardeners take what they can get. Fire escapes started appearing on tenement buildings in the 1860s and have become an indelible feature of the cityscape (think of Maria's balcony in *West Side Story*). They're many New Yorkers' only opportunity to flex their green thumbs on a fine June day. Celebrate the summer solstice with the Consulate of Sweden's **Midsummer Festival, yoga in Times Square**—or a simple glass of wine on your own verdant fire escape. Celebrate Pride month with the **Pride March** or **Harlem Pride** festival, and try to hit all eight participating museums during the **Museum Mile Festival**. June is also the last chance to visit NYPL's Schomberg Center for **an exhibition celebrating its 100th anniversary**.

OUTLOOK: *Ready or not, it's finally hot. But don't forget your umbrella—there could be a chance thunderstorm, fella. The Belmont Stakes on the 6th will be run on a dry track. School kids must endure final exams and, for the balance of the month, it will be hot and sticky for arithmeticky. The heat will mostly be dry . . . feels like July. Still a potential for torrential pop-up showers.*

NORMALS FOR CENTRAL PARK	Although three of the last five months of 2024 were slightly cooler than average, temperatures for the first seven months spiked so high that it ended up being NYC's second warmest year on record. (City weather records date all the way back to 1869.) The warmest year, 2023, held on to its #1 position by a mere 0.03°. The year 2024 also had the fourth warmest winter and the fourth warmest spring.
Average High: 79.7° Average Low: 64.4° Average Liquid Precipitation: 4.54"	

Sky Watch: A fascinating dance of three planets and the Moon provide evening enchantment this month. One hour after sunset on June 9, the brightest planets, Venus and Jupiter, call attention to themselves low in the west-northwest sky. On the 16th, a slender crescent Moon appears to the right of Jupiter, and below the Moon sits a third planet, Mercury. The following evening, the lunar crescent passes just off to the left of Venus.

ANNALS OF THE NIGHT SKY

Thanks to the spread of light pollution over the past half century, it is estimated that approximately 90 percent of Americans have never seen the Milky Way, and 80 percent have difficulty seeing stars near their homes. If you're interested in taking steps to reduce extra nighttime lighting in your own town, consider joining Dark Sky International. Founded in 1988, Dark Sky has played a pivotal role in turning the tide in the war against light pollution. For more information, go to darksky.org.

NYC BOOK OF THE MONTH
Broadway for Paul by Vincent Katz (2020)

"I am totally enamored of every person passing in this unseasonably warm mid-March evening near 39th and Park," writes Katz in the poem "Between the Griffon and Met Life." Katz, who's been called a "21st-century flaneur," takes readers on a walk around the city as only a born-and-bred New Yorker could. "I'll complain," he writes, "but I'll never leave."

NYC MOVIE OF THE MONTH
Street Scene, directed by King Vidor, written by Elmer Rice, starring Estelle Taylor, Sylvia Sidney, and William Collier Jr. (1931)

Street Scene is set on the stoop of a Hell's Kitchen walk-up during a summer heat wave. The melodramatic, pre-Code plot centers on a double murder, offering a glimpse of one small slice of the Depression-era city based on Rice's Pulitzer Prize–winning play. Busybody neighbors lean out over windowsills, and crowds gather to gawk. Alfred Newman's score was so evocative of the city, it was used in seven 1940s films.

# Jun. 1–7

"And though it's messy in the street, / The sky above is large and neat. / And from this fire escape of mine / The cloud effects are very fine."
—Margaret Fishback

1 MONDAY
☼ 5:27 AM / 8:21 PM

New York City Independent Film Festival (through Jun. 7)

2 TUESDAY
☼ 5:26 AM / 8:21 PM

Orchestra of St. Luke's at Carnegie Hall

3 WEDNESDAY
☼ 5:26 AM / 8:22 PM

Tribeca Film Festival (through Jun. 14)

4 THURSDAY
☼ 5:25 AM / 8:23 PM

Semyon Bychkov Conducts Bruckner's Eighth, New York Philharmonic (Jun. 4–6)

5 FRIDAY
☼ 5:25 AM / 8:23 PM

Etienne Charles: Folklore Live Vol. 2 at Jazz at Lincoln Center (and Jun. 6)

6 SATURDAY
☼ 5:25 AM / 8:24 PM

D-Day

Last chance to see *Turandot* at the Metropolitan Opera

7 SUNDAY
☼ 5:25 AM / 8:25 PM

New Queens Pride Parade, Jackson Heights, Queens

Jun. 8–14

"The sun fell across them and across the fire escape with a high, benevolent indifference; below them, men and women, boys and girls, sinners all, loitered."
—James Baldwin

8 MONDAY

☼ 5:24 AM / 8:25 PM   ◐ 1ST QUARTER

2009: First section of the High Line opens

9 TUESDAY

☼ 5:24 AM / 8:26 PM

Carnegie Hall presents *An Evening with Isabel Leonard and Friends*

10 WEDNESDAY

☼ 5:24 AM / 8:26 PM

1928: Maurice Sendak is born in Brooklyn

11 THURSDAY

☼ 5:24 AM / 8:27 PM

Carnegie Hall presents the Met Orchestra

12 FRIDAY

☼ 5:24 AM / 8:27 PM

Hamilton de Holand and the Music of Moacir Santos at Jazz at Lincoln Center (and Jun. 13)

13 SATURDAY

☼ 5:24 AM / 8:28 PM

1962: Actor Ally Sheedy is born in New York City

14 SUNDAY

☼ 5:24 AM / 8:28 PM

Flag Day
National Puerto Rican Day Parade

Jun. 15–21

"She... climbed out on the fire escape. Once there, she was living in a tree. No one downstairs, or across the way could see her. But she could look out through the leaves and see everything."
—Betty Smith

---

15 MONDAY

☼ 5:24 AM / 8:28 PM ● NEW MOON

1915: Jazz guitarist Allan Reuss (who played with Benny Goodman) is born in New York

---

16 TUESDAY

☼ 5:24 AM / 8:29 PM

Islamic New Year

Catch *Face Value: Celebrity Press Photography* at the Museum of Modern Art before it closes on Jun. 21

---

17 WEDNESDAY

☼ 5:24 AM / 8:29 PM

City Center Encores! Presents *La Cage Aux Folles* with Billy Porter (Jun. 17–28)

---

18 THURSDAY

☼ 5:24 AM / 8:29 PM

Blues Jam at Jazz at Lincoln Center (through Jun. 20)

---

19 FRIDAY

☼ 5:24 AM / 8:30 PM

Swedish Midsummer Festival presented by the Consulate General of Sweden

---

20 SATURDAY

☼ 5:24 AM / 8:30 PM

New York Philharmonic presents *Disney's Encanto in Concert* (Jun. 18–21)

---

21 SUNDAY

☼ 5:25 AM / 8:30 PM ◐ 1ST QUARTER

♋ CANCER

Summer Solstice
Father's Day

Practice yoga at the Solstice in Times Square

Jun. 22–28

"New York runs a red light past sentiment."
 —Sasha Frere-Jones

22 MONDAY

☼ 5:25 AM / 8:30 PM

1953: Cyndi Lauper is born in Brooklyn

23 TUESDAY

☼ 5:25 AM / 8:31 PM

Democracy Matters at the New York Historical (opens Jun. 19)

24 WEDNESDAY

☼ 5:25 AM / 8:31 PM

New York Philharmonic presents *Star Wars: Return of the Jedi In Concert* (through Jun. 27)

25 THURSDAY

☼ 5:26 AM / 8:31 PM

Summer Evenings in the Garden, with music and guided tours, at the Merchant's House Museum (Thursdays Jun.–Jul.)

26 FRIDAY

☼ 5:26 AM / 8:31 PM

New York City Public Schools—last day of school

27 SATURDAY

☼ 5:26 AM / 8:31 PM

Harlem Pride Day Celebration

28 SUNDAY

☼ 5:27 AM / 8:31 PM

NYC Pride March

JULY

THIS POLYGLOT CITY of immigrants and outsiders, activists and artists, was once briefly the capital of the brand-new United States (following occupation by British forces during the Revolutionary War). George Washington bid farewell to his officers at Fraunces Tavern in 1783 and took the oath of office as the nation's first President at Federal Hall in 1789. This July 4, the city celebrates the **semiquincentennial of the United States**—and its own place in the history of the nation's founding. The largest-ever flotilla of tall ships from around the world will sail into New York Harbor from the Verrazzano Bridge to the George Washington Bridge. **Visit Revolutionary War sites** from Fraunces Tavern to Green-Wood Cemetery (where the Battle of Brooklyn took place) to Fort Greene Park (where more than 11,500 patriots are buried under the Prison Ship Martyrs Monument), or take the ferry to Sandy Hook, NJ, the British stronghold at the mouth of New York Harbor, to see the oldest operating lighthouse in the US, built by the British in 1764.

OUTLOOK: *First few days of July are hot and showery, then fine weather arrives just in time for the Fabulous Fourth and continues for several days beyond. From the 12th through the 15th, beware of thunderstorms capable of localized drown-pours and dangerous lightning; that's an "atmos-fear." Final ten days of July see frequent showers; it's one damp thing after another.*

NORMALS FOR
CENTRAL PARK
Average High: 84.9°
Average Low: 70.1°
Average Liquid
Precipitation: 4.60"

Officially, New York City's hottest day was ninety years ago on July 9, 1936, when the Central Park temperature topped off at 106°. However, thirty years later, on July 3, 1966, La Guardia Airport recorded a high of 107°—1° above the all-time record, which still stands. On that sweltering day in 1966, Central Park hit 103° and Kennedy Airport topped off at 104°.

Sky Watch: On July 9, Venus passes less than one degree above the bluish star Regulus in Leo the Lion. If you're an early riser, look low to the east-northeast horizon an hour before sunrise on July 11 to see an alignment of a crescent Moon, Mars, and the orange star Aldebaran. Although widely separated, the Moon and Venus still make for an eye-catching pair on the evening of the 18th.

ANNALS OF THE NIGHT SKY

In a single year, light travels 5.88 trillion miles—or one *light year*, a unit that astronomers use to measure stellar distances. When you look at a star, you're seeing it not as it is, but as it was. The starlight reaching your eyes began its journey to Earth several years ago at least. On July 20, look above the moon to see the star Spica. The light you're seeing started traveling here 250 years ago, around the time the Declaration of Independence was adopted unanimously by the Second Continental Congress.

NYC BOOK OF THE MONTH

Tenements, Towers & Trash: An Unconventional Illustrated History of New York City by Julia Wertz (2017)

Comic artist Julia Wertz takes readers beyond the tourist's New York and into the shadows of the city's past—which are still present, if you look close enough. She tells the story of Kim's Video, the Ray's Pizza wars, and Madame Restell—the abortionist of Fifth Avenue—with a mix of wonder, humor, and nostalgia. Wertz wrote the book in California after being priced out of her beloved city.

NYC MOVIE OF THE MONTH

In the Heights, directed by Jon M. Chu, starring Anthony Ramos, Corey Hawkins, Leslie Grace, and others (2021)

Filmed entirely on location in Washington Heights, this adaptation of Lin-Manuel Miranda's hit musical features a 500-person Busby Berkeley-style dance number filmed over two days at Highbridge Pool on Amsterdam and 171st Street. In another number, Abuela Claudia time-travels as she sings through vintage subway cars and finally the graffiti-lined, 1,000-foot tunnel in the 191st Street subway station.

Jun. 29–Jul. 5

"On the first Saturday of a city summer... Central Park, as public as an ocean, became, in effect, the city's rumpus room."
—Bruce Weber

29 MONDAY
☼ 5:27 AM / 8:31 PM ○ FULL MOON

1855: The first known advertisement for Walt Whitman's *Leaves of Grass* appears in the *Brooklyn Daily Eagle*

30 TUESDAY
☼ 5:28 AM / 8:31 PM

Last Chance to see *100: A Century of Collections, Community, and Creativity* at NYPL's Schomburg Center

1 WEDNESDAY
☼ 5:28 AM / 8:31 PM

1972: First issue of *Ms.* magazine is published

2 THURSDAY
☼ 5:29 AM / 8:30 PM

1951: Gay rights and transgender activist Sylvia Rivera is born in New York City

3 FRIDAY
☼ 5:29 AM / 8:30 PM

Tall ships with Sail4th 250 anchor at Sandy Hook, NJ, the gateway to New York Harbor, and Class B ships parade on the East River

4 SATURDAY
☼ 5:30 AM / 8:30 PM

Independence Day

Sail4th 250 Parade of Tall Ships from the Verrazano Bridge to the George Washington Bridge in celebration of the US Semiquincentennial

5 SUNDAY
☼ 5:30 AM / 8:30 PM

Last chance to see *Artist's Choice: Arthur Jafa—Less Is Morbid* at the Museum of Modern Art

Jul. 6–12

"I spend the whole walk in the current New York City looking for evidence of the past New York City."
—Julia Wertz

6 MONDAY

☼ 5:31 AM / 8:29 PM

1928: Ticker tape parade for Amelia Earhart, Wilmer Stultz, and Louis E. Gordon following their transatlantic flight

7 TUESDAY

☼ 5:32 AM / 8:29 PM   ☽ 3RD QUARTER

1952: Ticker tape parade for the US Olympic team

8 WEDNESDAY

☼ 5:32 AM / 8:29 PM

1889: First issue of the *Wall Street Journal* is published

9 THURSDAY

☼ 5:33 AM / 8:28 PM

1776: George Washington reads the Declaration of Independence to his troops

10 FRIDAY

☼ 5:34 AM / 8:28 PM

1947: Folk singer Arlo Guthrie is born in Brooklyn

11 SATURDAY

☼ 5:34 AM / 8:28 PM

1974: Lil' Kim is born in Brooklyn

12 SUNDAY

☼ 5:35 AM / 8:27 PM

Last chance to see *The Many Lives of the Nakagin Capsule Tower* at the Museum of Modern Art

Jul. 13–19

"I have been living in New York for twenty-two years and still get the weird feeling that I am living in a dream. Not living *a dream*... but inhabiting a blur of the fictional and the real."
—E. Tammy Kim

13 MONDAY
☼ 5:36 AM / 8:27 PM

1925: A record 800,000 people visit Coney Island

14 TUESDAY
☼ 5:37 AM / 8:26 PM ● NEW MOON

Bastille Day

15 WEDNESDAY
☼ 5:37 AM / 8:25 PM

1938: Ticker tape parade for Howard Hughes following a three-day flight around the world

16 THURSDAY
☼ 5:38 AM / 8:25 PM

1776: Patriots take down a statue of George III in Bowling Green after a reading of the Declaration of Independence

17 FRIDAY
☼ 5:39 AM / 8:24 PM

1899: Actor James Cagney is born on the Lower East Side

18 SATURDAY
☼ 5:40 AM / 8:23 PM

1908: The Frogs, an African-American theatrical organization, is founded in Harlem

19 SUNDAY
☼ 5:41 AM / 8:23 PM

Celebrate National Ice Cream Day at Ample Hills Creamery in Brooklyn

Jul. 20–26

"The city's chaos germs lurk in the soil itself. Developers are just building future ruins."
—Lucy Sante

20 MONDAY

☼ 5:41 AM / 8:22 PM

1849: Robert Anderson Van Wyck—the first mayor of New York after consolidation of the five-borough city—is born in New York City

21 TUESDAY

☼ 5:42 AM / 8:21 PM ◐ 1ST QUARTER

1933: Ticker tape parade for Air Marshal Italo Balbo and crew

22 WEDNESDAY

☼ 5:43 AM / 8:20 PM ♌ LEO

1884: "Marm" Mandelbaum, the Lower East Side's "Queen of Thieves," is arrested in her shop at Clinton and Rivington Streets.

23 THURSDAY

☼ 5:44 AM / 8:20 PM

Hugo Marchand: Artists at the Center at New York City Center (through Jul. 25)

24 FRIDAY

☼ 5:45 AM / 8:19 PM

1969: Jennifer Lopez is born in the Bronx

25 SATURDAY

☼ 5:46 AM / 8:18 PM

1914: Eldridge Street. between Rivington and Delancey closes to traffic for the first "play street"

26 SUNDAY

☼ 5:47 AM / 8:17 PM

1933: Ticker tape parade for Wiley Post following his eight-day around-the-world flight

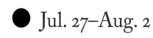
Jul. 27–Aug. 2

"Central Park is a synthetic Arcadian Carpet."
—Rem Koolhaus

27 MONDAY
☼ 5:48 AM / 8:16 PM

1905: Leo Durocher, Brooklyn Dodgers manager from 1939 to 1946, is born in West Springfield, MA

28 TUESDAY
☼ 5:49 AM / 8:15 PM   ○ FULL MOON

1917: NAACP organizes a silent march to protest lynching

29 WEDNESDAY
☼ 5:50 AM / 8:14 PM   ○ FULL MOON

David Ostwald's Louis Armstrong Eternity Band at Birdland jazz club (Wednesdays)

30 THURSDAY
☼ 5:50 AM / 8:13 PM

The High Society New Orleans Jazz Band at Birdland jazz club (Thursdays)

31 FRIDAY
☼ 5:51 AM / 8:12 PM

1904: Arthur Daley, Pulitzer Prize–winning sportswriter, is born in New York City

1 SATURDAY
☼ 5:52 AM / 8:11 PM

Afternoon Ghost Tour at the Merchant's House Museum (first Saturday of the month, Feb.–Sep.)

2 SUNDAY
☼ 5:53 AM / 8:10 PM

Open Mic night at Pete's Candy Store (Sundays)

AUGUST

IN THE LIMINAL DARKNESS of summer evenings, when the sun has set behind the tallest buildings (but not quite behind the horizon), the city's parks transform, playing host to curious raccoons, twinkling fireflies—and sometimes abrupt downpours. While you wait for **an outdoor movie in Bryant Park or Astoria Park**, or performances by the hippest bands in **Prospect Park's Bandshell**, look closely and the grit of the city will melt away. A certain permissiveness pervades the atmosphere as wine is poured into plastic cups, bare feet stretch out on picnic blankets, and sleepy, sunburned revelers begin the long trek back by subway from Coney Island or ferry from the Rockaways. Take advantage of summer nights as **Lincoln Center's Summer for the City** festival wraps up, Governor's Island hosts the **Jazz Age Lawn Party**, and the **Charlie Parker Jazz Festival** brings up-and-coming players to neighborhoods where Parker lived and played.

OUTLOOK: *First half of this month turns muggier and buggier. Have a cookout, then look out! Temperatures couldn't get much higher; out of the frying pan and into the fire. Hot and humid. Stray thunderboomers are rumored. Can it get any worse? How about a hurricane threat around the 21st? The eye of a hurricane is a void you should avoid. Beg your pardon, but the final week of August is sodden.*

NORMALS FOR
CENTRAL PARK
Average High: 83.3°
Average Low: 68.9°
Average Liquid
Precipitation: 4.56"

Fifty years ago, in the early hours of August 10, 1976, Hurricane Belle paid a visit to the Tri-State area. The storm cut a path all the way from Long Beach to Lloyd's Neck-Oyster Bay. In NYC, winds reached 60 m.p.h., bringing heavy, squally rains. In Westchester, the storm caused thousands of blackouts; across parts of central and eastern Long Island, winds gusted to 115 m.p.h. The worst was over by 1:30 a.m.

Sky Watch: Early on the morning of the 12th, the annual Perseid meteor shower will reach its peak. If you can get away from bright city lights, you'll be rewarded every so often by meteors darting out of the northeast sky. Later that day, from 1:07 to 2:38 p.m., a minor (less than 10 percent) partial solar eclipse occurs—not worth putting your eyes at risk for. But on August 28, an "almost total" lunar eclipse takes place. At 12:12 a.m., 93 percent of the Moon will be immersed in Earth's shadow.

ANNALS OF THE NIGHT SKY

Our Sun is only one of an estimated 400 billion stars in the Milky Way galaxy and is considered an "average" star in terms of size and luminosity. The largest star visible to the naked eye is Mu Cephi, in the constellation of Cepheus the King: a dim star so strikingly red that the eighteenth-century astronomer William Herschel called it the Garnet Star. If our Sun were the size of a softball, Mu, in comparison, would be a globe 437 feet across!

NYC BOOK OF THE MONTH
Rat Bohemia by Sarah Schulman (1995)

Schulman's protagonist, Rita, was born on August 1, 1959, in Jackson Heights, Queens. As a young woman, Rita confronts and bears witness to the devastation of the AIDS epidemic. Reviewing the book for the *Times,* Edmund White wrote of Schulman, "The force of her indignation is savage and has blown the traditional novel off its hinges. If she were contributing to the quilt project, her quilt would be on fire."

NYC MOVIE OF THE MONTH
The Seven Year Itch, directed by Billy Wilder, starring Marilyn Monroe and Tom Ewell (1955)

Monroe's turn as the unnamed "Girl" is riveting as she plays into—and pokes fun at—a certain "type" of young, unmarried New York woman. The movie also features one of the most iconic scenes in American film history (white dress, subway grate), filmed on Lexington Avenue.

Aug. 3–9

"It's one of life's little ironies that in New York, a gastronomic paradise, the classic of classics is the lowly hot dog, served from a street cart. Nestled in a bun, topped with mustard, onions, and sauerkraut."
—William Grimes

---

3 MONDAY

☼ 5:54 AM / 8:09 PM

1920: Jazz trumpet player Charlie Shavers is born in New York City

---

4 TUESDAY

☼ 5:55 AM / 8:07 PM

Silent Writing Happy Hour at Pete's Candy Store (Tuesdays)

---

5 WEDNESDAY

☼ 5:56 AM / 8:06 PM

1867: Jacob Ruppert Jr., owner of the Yankees from 1915 to 1939, is born in New York City

---

6 THURSDAY

☼ 5:57 AM / 8:05 PM
☽ 3RD QUARTER

1981: *Rolling Stone* calls West 42nd Street "the sleaziest block in America"

---

7 FRIDAY

☼ 5:58 AM / 8:04 PM

Dead Pete's Society open-mic poetry at Pete's Candy Store (first Friday of the month)

---

8 SATURDAY

☼ 5:59 AM / 8:03PM

Queens Night Market at the New York Hall of Science in Flushing Meadows Park (Saturdays, Apr.–Oct.)

---

9 SUNDAY

☼ 6:00 AM / 8:01 PM

1959: Kurtis Blow is born in Harlem

Aug. 10–16

"It's not true New Yorkers have no heart; we've got trees and rivers and fossils and hills and nature all around us, and there's no reason to live anywhere else."
—Terry Clifford

---

10 MONDAY

☼ 6:01 AM / 8:00 PM

1970: McSorley's manager Daniel O'Connell-Kirwan reluctantly admits the bar's first woman customer, Barbara Shaum

---

11 TUESDAY

☼ 6:02 AM / 7:59 PM

1972: Polish-born labor leader Rose Schneiderman dies at age ninety in New York City

---

12 WEDNESDAY

☼ 6:03 AM / 7:57 PM ● NEW MOON

International Puppet Fringe Festival of New York (IPFFNYC) at the Clemente (through Aug. 16)

---

13 THURSDAY

☼ 6:04 AM / 7:56 PM

1969: Ticker tape parade for Neil Armstrong, Buzz Aldrin, and Michael Collins following the Apollo 11 mission to the Moon

---

14 FRIDAY

☼ 6:05 AM / 7:55 PM

Birdland Big Band at Birdland jazz club (Fridays)

---

15 SATURDAY

☼ 6:06 AM / 7:53 PM

1965: The Beatles play Shea Stadium—the first concert held in a baseball stadium

---

16 SUNDAY

☼ 6:07 AM / 7:52 PM

Feast of Saint Rocco

1824: At least 200,000 New Yorkers welcome the Marquis de Lafayette with a parade

Aug. 17–23

"How funny you are today New York / like Ginger Rogers in *Swingtime*... oh god it's wonderful / to get out of bed / and drink too much coffee / and smoke too many cigarettes / and love you so much."
—Frank O'Hara

---

17 MONDAY
☼ 6:08 AM / 7:51 PM

1807: Robert Fulton's first American steamboat leaves New York City for Albany

---

18 TUESDAY
☼ 6:09 AM / 7:49 PM

1981: Anita Loos, writer of *Gentlemen Prefer Blondes*, dies in New York at age ninety-three

---

19 WEDNESDAY
☼ 6:10 AM / 7:48 PM

1949: Ticker tape parade for Connie Mack, celebrating his fiftieth anniversary as manager of the Philadelphia Athletics

---

20 THURSDAY
☼ 6:11 AM / 7:46 PM
☽ 1ST QUARTER

1954: Weatherman Al Roker is born in Queens

---

21 FRIDAY
☼ 6:12 AM / 7:45 PM

1929: Herman Badillo, who represented the South Bronx in the US House, is born in Puerto Rico

---

22 SATURDAY
☼ 6:13 AM / 7:43 PM

1776: British General Howe lands 22,000 troops at Gravesend Bay—the start of the Revolutionary War's New York campaign

---

23 SUNDAY
☼ 6:14 AM / 7:42 PM ♍ VIRGO

1943: *LIFE* magazine publishes a photo spread titled "*LIFE* Visits McSorley's Old Ale House"

Aug. 24–30

"Sometimes our affection for New York becomes dulled by familiarity.... Then in a moment of rediscovery, it is as though we were meeting the city again for the first time."
—E. B. White

---

24 MONDAY
☼ 6:15 AM / 7:40 PM

1945: Activist Marsha P. Johnson is born in Elizabeth, New Jersey

---

25 TUESDAY
☼ 6:16 AM / 7:39 PM

1931: Regis Philbin is born in Manhattan

---

26 WEDNESDAY
☼ 6:17 AM / 7:37 PM

Celebrate National Dog Day with the New York Dog Parade

---

27 THURSDAY
☼ 6:18 AM / 7:36 PM

1776: Revolutionary War Battle of Long Island, a.k.a. Battle of Brooklyn

---

28 FRIDAY
☼ 6:19 AM / 7:34 PM

1945: Jackie Robinson meets with Brooklyn Dodgers general manager Branch Rickey and signs a contract to play for Brooklyn's farm team, the Montreal Royals

---

29 SATURDAY
☼ 6:20 AM / 7:32 PM

Bronx Night Market at Fordham Plaza (last Saturday of the month, Apr.–Oct.)

---

30 SUNDAY
☼ 6:21 AM / 7:31 PM

The Afro Latin Jazz Orchestra at Birdland jazz club (Sundays)

SEPTEMBER

As summer's laziness fades to something more like boredom, the fall season steps up with high-energy events: from the **Labor Day Parade** (showcasing the solidarity of the city's labor unions) to the **West Indian Day Parade** (celebrating Caribbean heritage) to Brooklyn's **Atlantic Antic** (the oldest and largest street festival in the borough) to Bushwick's **Open Studios** festival (featuring galleries, studios, storefronts, music venues, and its very own zine) to the massive **Armory Show** bringing art from all over the world to the Javits Center. Meanwhile, the city's many galleries and museums launch blockbuster exhibitions for the can't-miss fall exhibition season. Time to pull out that fall coat for the three days when it's appropriate, enjoy the nips of cool weather, and admire autumn foliage throughout the city's parks.

Outlook: *This month kicks off warm and hazy; it makes one lazy. Sadly, for the final summer holiday weekend, we anticipate gray, dreary skies; such chicanery, cool and rainy. Hate to mention you might get a drenchin'. Then for September's second week, more rain. Hurricane? Just in time for the equinox, it's windy and wet—a storm we'll get. Northeast gales come down the vales. At last! In the final week, a blue sky and the weather dry.*

Normals for Central Park	
Average High: 76.2° Average Low: 62.3° Average Liquid Precipitation: 4.31"	The Mid-Atlantic hurricane of 1936 was a historic near-miss for NYC. The eye of this category 2 storm passed within 50 miles of the Virginia coast on September 18, then rapidly curved away from the mainland US. Nonetheless, it came close enough to NYC the following morning to bring a steady and at times blinding heavy rain amounting to over 3", accompanied by northeast gales that uprooted trees, crippled shipping, and grounded aircraft.

SKY WATCH: At the break of dawn on September 6, a wide crescent Moon hovers well above Mars, which appears as a yellow-orange star. Two mornings later, on the 8th, a somewhat thinner crescent Moon lies a similar distance above another, far more brilliant planet, Jupiter. The autumnal equinox occurs at 8:05 p.m. on the 23rd, and the full Moon occurring closest to the start of fall, a.k.a. the Harvest Moon, appears on the 26th.

ANNALS OF THE NIGHT SKY

In 1850, the very first photograph of a star was taken at Harvard College Observatory. The star in question was bluish Vega, fifth brightest in the sky, and currently soaring almost directly overhead at nightfall. If you want to try your own hand at astrophotography, check to see if your smartphone camera includes a night mode that lets you record exposures of several seconds or more. Adding a tripod with a smartphone bracket and a Bluetooth shutter trigger will improve your results.

NYC BOOK OF THE MONTH
Going into Town: A Love Letter to New York by Roz Chast (2017)

From the start, Chast promises that *Going into Town* is not a guidebook, not an insider's guide, and definitely not a history book. It began as a relatively straightforward instruction manual for her daughter, who was leaving the suburbs for college in Manhattan, but it grew into a book just as particular (and somehow still universal) as her best *New Yorker* cartoons.

NYC MOVIE OF THE MONTH
The Paper, directed by Ron Howard, starring Michael Keaton, Glenn Close, Marisa Tomei, Randy Quaid, and Robert Duvall (1994)

Striving for realism in this slightly old-school, one-day-at-work newspaper film, Ron Howard visited newsrooms at the *New York Post* and *Daily News*; met with Pete Hamill (who makes a cameo) and Jimmy Breslin; and modeled Keaton's character on real-life reporter Richie Esposito. Viewed today, it triggers nostalgia for a time when the truth could be read in black and white, and print media truly mattered.

Aug. 31–Sep. 6

"My experience as a young New York reporter... prepared me to be astonished by virtually nothing."
—Gay Talese

31 MONDAY

☼ 6:22 AM / 7:29 PM

US Open Tennis tournament begins at the Billie Jean King National Tennis Center in Flushing, Queens.

1 TUESDAY

☼ 6:23 AM / 7:28 PM

1932: Mayor Jimmy Walker resigns amid scandal and the threat of criminal indictment

2 WEDNESDAY

☼ 6:24 AM / 7:26 PM

1942: Choreographer Ned Wayburn dies in New York City

3 THURSDAY

☼ 6:25 AM / 7:24 PM

1936: Ticker tape parade for Jesse Owens following his four gold medals at the 1936 Summer Olympics

4 FRIDAY

☼ 6:26 AM / 7:23 PM   ☽ 3RD QUARTER

1882: Thomas Edison powers Wall Street with the first underground electric system in the US

5 SATURDAY

☼ 6:27 AM / 7:21 PM

Richmond County Fair at Historic Richmond Town, Staten Island (through Sep. 7)

6 SUNDAY

☼ 6:28 AM / 7:19 PM

1978: Foxy Brown is born in Brooklyn

Sep. 7–13

"If you are paying $65 or $75... you are seeing an Off-Broadway show. If you are fanning yourself with your program and wondering about fire code violations, it's definitely a double-Off experience."
—Charles Isherwood

---

7 MONDAY
☼ 6:29 AM / 7:18 PM

Labor Day

West Indian Carnival (and J'ouvert) in Crown Heights, Brooklyn

---

8 TUESDAY
☼ 6:29 AM / 7:16 PM

1919: Ticker tape parade for General John J. Pershing

---

9 WEDNESDAY
☼ 6:30 AM / 7:14 PM

1941: Joan Baez is born in Staten Island

---

10 THURSDAY
☼ 6:31 AM / 7:13 PM

Uptown Night Market under the Arches of Harlem, 133 Street and Twelfth Avenue, West Harlem (second Thursdays Apr.–Oct.)

---

11 FRIDAY
☼ 6:32 AM / 7:11 PM ● NEW MOON

Rosh Hashanah begins.

Commemorations of the World Trade Center attack at the 9/11 Memorial

---

12 SATURDAY
☼ 6:33 AM / 7:09 PM

1896: Siegel-Cooper department store opens on Broadway between 18th and 19th Streets

---

13 SUNDAY
☼ 6:34 AM / 7:08 PM

Rosh Hashanah ends.

1970: The first New York City Marathon

Sep. 14–20

"CBGB is a state of mind. When I go into a rock club in Helsinki or London or Des Moines, it feels like CBGB."
—Lenny Kaye

14 MONDAY

☼ 6:35 AM / 7:06 PM

Vanguard Jazz Orchestra at the Village Vanguard (Mondays)

15 TUESDAY

☼ 6:36 AM / 7:04 PM

1776: The Revolutionary War Battle of Kip's Bay

16 WEDNESDAY

☼ 6:37 AM / 7:03 PM

1776: The Revolutionary War Battle of Harlem Heights

17 THURSDAY ●

☼ 6:38 AM / 7:01 PM

2011: Occupy Wall Street begins

18 FRIDAY

☼ 6:39 AM / 6:59 PM   ◐ 1ST QUARTER

1960: Fidel Castro arrives in New York as head of the Cuban delegation to the UN

19 SATURDAY

☼ 6:40 AM / 6:58 PM

Feast of San Gennaro

German-American Steuben Parade, Fifth Ave.

20 SUNDAY

☼ 6:41 AM / 6:56 PM

1970: A sit-in at NYU's Weinstein Hall inspires Marsha P. Johnson to start the Street Transvestite Action Revolutionaries (STAR)

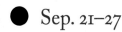# Sep. 21–27

"If the day does not begin with the New York newspapers, it has no foundation."
—Brooks Atkinson

24 THURSDAY
☼ 6:45 AM / 6:49 PM

1941: Linda McCartney is born in Manhattan

21 MONDAY
☼ 6:42 AM / 6:54 PM

Yom Kippur

1776: Nearly a quater of the city's buildings burn to the ground six days after British occupation

25 FRIDAY
☼ 6:46 AM / 6:47 PM

Sukkot begins.

1917: Yankee Phil Rizzuto is born in Brooklyn

22 TUESDAY
☼ 6:43 AM / 6:53 PM   ♎ LIBRA

Autumnal Equinox

1830: Caroline Schermerhorn Astor, whose ballroom held the famous "Four Hundred," is born

26 SATURDAY
☼ 6:47 AM / 6:46 PM   ○ FULL MOON

Tone's Bluegrass Jam at Sunny's Bar in Red Hook, Brooklyn (Saturdays)

23 WEDNESDAY
☼ 6:44 AM / 6:51 PM

Funhouse Comedy show at Pete's Candy Store (Wednesdays)

27 SUNDAY
☼ 6:48 AM / 6:44 PM

1888: The thirteen-story Tower Building, the first to be built with a steel skeleton, opens

Sep. 28–Oct. 4

"Whenever I go to Williamsburg...
I feel like I've missed a memo on
the proper width for pant legs."
 —Nicole Rifkin

28 MONDAY

☼ 6:49 AM / 6:42 PM

1951: Ticker tape parade for Alcide De Gasperi, prime minister of Italy

29 TUESDAY

☼ 6:50 AM / 6:41 PM

1954: The New York Giants' Willie Mays makes "The Catch"—an over-the-shoulder grab of a fly ball deep into center field—in Game 1 of the World Series

30 WEDNESDAY

☼ 6:51 AM / 6:39 PM

1899: Ticker tape parade for Admiral George Dewey following his return from Manila

1 THURSDAY

☼ 6:52 AM / 6:37 PM

1929: The original Waldorf Astoria hotel is razed

2 FRIDAY

☼ 6:53 AM / 6:36 PM

Sukkot ends.

You Should Be Dancing: New York, 1976 opens at the New York Historical

3 SATURDAY

☼ 6:54 AM / 6:34 PM   ☽ 3RD QUARTER

Pumpkin picking at Historic Richmond Town's Decker Farm (Saturdays and Sundays through Oct.)

4 SUNDAY

☼ 6:55 AM / 6:33 PM

Atlantic Antic, Brooklyn's oldest and largest street fair

OCTOBER

THE SOPHISTICATED SILLINESS of New Yorkers is on full display during the Halloween season—from elaborate stoop displays to clever of-the-moment costumes for kids, adults, and pups, too. You can pretend you live in the country or the dreaded suburbs by **picking pumpkins in Governor's Island, Historic Richmond Town's Decker Farm, or the Queens County Farm Museum**. Stone Street—always the spot for suit-wearing finance types to cut loose—turns into a German beer garden on Saturdays in September and October, with live music, stein-holding competitions, and of course, beer. The Bohemian Hall and Beer Garden in Astoria, Queens—established in 1910 and still operated by the Bohemian Citizens' Benevolent Society of Astoria—is an authentic way to **celebrate beer-drinking season**. Famous, and normally inaccessible, city buildings throw open their doors for **Archtober**, while the literati get their fill of writing, performance, and politics during the **New Yorker Festival**.

OUTLOOK: *Nothing sober this October. It starts a little snappier to make you happier. But during the second week, what luck; it rains a bucket. Afterward there's a movement toward improvement, but by the 19th, the barometer is dropping, and soon it's sopping. And by month's end, it's more of a trick than a treat: storm clouds usher in another gusher. Boo!*

NORMALS FOR
CENTRAL PARK
Average High: 64.5°
Average Low: 51.4°
Average Liquid
Precipitation: 4.38"
Average Snowfall: 0.1"

In 155 years of record-keeping, Central Park has never seen a month when no measurable precipitation fell. But October 2024 came awfully close. Typically, we can expect over 4" of rain in October, but in 2024, the only day that month with any precipitation was the 29th—a paltry 0.01". That sprinkle broke a stretch of twenty-nine straight dry days. The old record was set in June 1949, when just 0.02" drizzled down.

Sky Watch: A spectacular celestial event is set to occur before dawn on October 6: Jupiter will be hidden by a lovely crescent Moon. Such a spectacle is quite rare: the last occurrence was in 2004; the next will be in 2038. You can watch Jupiter disappear at 4:24 a.m. using no optical aid at all—although binoculars will give a better view. The planet's reappearance at 5:27 a.m. should be quite dramatic, resembling a brightening jewel on the dark limb of the Moon.

ANNALS OF THE NIGHT SKY

The largest object currently circling Earth is the International Space Station (ISS). It's also the brightest, sometimes shining as intensely as Venus, so even from brightly lit Manhattan you can see it if you know when and where to look. For a specific schedule as to when it will be passing over your neighborhood, go to spotthestation.nasa.gov.

NYC BOOK OF THE MONTH
Paul Auster's The New York Trilogy, adapted by Paul Karasik, Lorenzo Mattotti, and David Mazzucchelli (2025)

Three distinguished graphic artists reinvent Auster's postmodern take on the noir detective novel, layering one work of genius on top of another. As the book opens, a tenement building façade morphs into a maze, while the text reads, "New York was a labyrinth of endless steps... and no matter how far he walked, it always left him with the feeling of being lost."

NYC MOVIE OF THE MONTH
Saving Face, directed by Alice Wu, starring Michelle Krusiec, Joan Chen, and Lynn Chen (2004)

Wu called her first full-length film "an Asian-American lesbian romantic comedy." Location shots include East Buffet & Restaurant in Flushing, Queens, and the pre-renovation TWA Terminal at JFK. Wu refused to change the race or sexuality of the main characters and got her establishing shot—a D train on the Manhattan Bridge—by hitching a ride on the helicopter filming Manhattan aerials for the big-budget movie *Hitch*.

Oct. 5–11

"Look at the common, ordinary city—not the lofty, noble silvery vertical city but the vast, spread-out, sooty-gray and sooty-brown and sooty-red and sooty-pink horizontal city..."
—Joseph Mitchell

5 MONDAY
☼ 6:56 AM / 6:31 PM

1923: Ticker tape parade for David Lloyd George, former prime minister of the UK

6 TUESDAY
☼ 6:57 AM / 6:29 PM

1937: Joe DiMaggio dines at the Cotton Club after the Yankees win Game 1 of the World Series against the Giants

7 WEDNESDAY
☼ 6:58 AM / 6:28 PM

1765: The Stamp Act Congress meets in New York City

8 THURSDAY
☼ 6:59 AM / 6:26 PM

1964: Ticker tape parade for Diosdado Macapagal, president of the Philippines

9 FRIDAY
☼ 7:00 AM / 6:24 PM

1945: Ticker tape parade for Fleet Admiral Chester Nimitz

10 SATURDAY
☼ 7:01 AM / 6:23 PM   ● NEW MOON

Visit New York City's only corn maze, the Amazing Maize Maze, at Queens County Farm (Saturdays and Sundays, Sep.–Oct.)

11 SUNDAY
☼ 7:03 AM / 6:21 PM

1992: Cardi B is born in Washington Heights

Oct. 12–18

"I thought of the Apple as a rogue republic, a free port like Trieste or Casablanca in the days when they drew the effluvia of the seven seas. It made its own laws; its door stood open to all who dared enter."
—Lucy Sante

---

12 MONDAY
☼ 7:04 AM / 6:20 PM

Columbus Day
Indigenous People's Day

Columbus Day Parade on Fifth Avenue

Indigenous People's Day celebrations at the National Museum of the American Indian

---

13 TUESDAY
☼ 7:05 AM / 6:18 PM

1961: Ticker tape parade for Ibrahim Abboud, president of Sudan

---

14 WEDNESDAY
☼ 7:06 AM / 6:17 PM

1842: Croton Aqueduct brings fresh drinking water to the city

---

15 THURSDAY
☼ 7:07 AM / 6:15 PM

1920: Mario Puzo, author of *The Godfather*, is born in Manhattan

---

16 FRIDAY
☼ 7:08 AM / 6:14 PM

Open House New York Weekend (through Oct. 18)

---

17 SATURDAY
☼ 7:09 AM / 6:12 PM

1949: Ticker tape parade for Jawaharlal Nehru, prime minister of India

---

18 SUNDAY
☼ 7:10 AM / 6:11 PM ◐ 1ST QUARTER

1926: Ticker tape parade for Queen Marie of Romania

Oct. 19–25

"Living in New York City gives people real incentives to want things that nobody else wants ... changing your tastes to what other people don't want is your only hope of getting anything."
—Andy Warhol

19 MONDAY
☼ 7:11 AM / 6:09 PM

Play Date, readings of new plays by emerging playwrights, at Pete's Candy Store (third Monday of the month)

20 TUESDAY
☼ 7:12 AM / 6:08 PM

1953: Ticker tape parade for General Mark W. Clark

21 WEDNESDAY
☼ 7:13 AM / 6:06 PM

1959: Frank Lloyd Wright's Solomon R. Guggenheim Museum opens to the public

22 THURSDAY
☼ 7:15 AM / 6:05 PM

1931: Ticker tape parade for Pierre Laval, Prime Minister of France

23 FRIDAY
☼ 7:16 AM / 6:03 PM ♏ SCORPIO

1946: Ticker tape parade for delegates to the first plenary session of the UN General Assembly

24 SATURDAY
☼ 7:17 AM / 6:02 PM

Eros Ramazzotti at the Theater at Madison Square Garden

25 SUNDAY
☼ 7:18 AM / 6:01 PM

1916: Painter William Merritt Chase dies in New York

Oct. 26–Nov. 1

"The good thing about New York is the bars stay open until 4 a.m.; the bad thing is the bars stay open until 4 a.m.... What makes New York fun and interesting? That the bars stay open until 4 a.m."
—Janeane Garofalo

---

26 MONDAY

☼ 7:19 AM / 5:59 PM ○ FULL MOON

1958: Pan Am flies first transatlantic jet from New York to Paris

---

27 TUESDAY

☼ 7:20 AM / 5:58 PM

1945: Ticker tape parade for President Harry S. Truman

---

28 WEDNESDAY

☼ 7:21 AM / 5:57 PM

1886: Impromptu ticker tape parade for the brand-new Statue of Liberty

---

29 THURSDAY

☼ 7:22 AM / 5:55 PM

Red Hook's Barnacle Parade celebrates the neighborhood's resilience in the face of Hurricane Sandy

---

30 FRIDAY

☼ 7:24 AM / 5:54 PM

Candlelight Ghost Tour at the Merchant's House Museum (and Oct. 16–17, 23–24)

---

31 SATURDAY

☼ 7:25 AM / 5:53 PM

Halloween

Greenwich Village Halloween Parade

---

1 SUNDAY

☼ 6:26 AM / 4:52 PM ☽ 3RD QUARTER

Daylight saving time ends.

TCS New York City Marathon

NOVEMBER

SOME SAY NEW YORK has its own sense of humor: dry, sarcastic, ironic, quick-witted. The city has incubated comic talent from the vaudeville days to the birth of standup—in clubs like the Bitter End, where Joan Rivers and Richard Pryor performed early in their careers—to today's Upright Citizens' Brigade classes, where aspiring comics hone their improv technique, and, of course, *Saturday Night Live*, which has been skewering pieties and politicians for fifty-one years. In mid-November, the **New York Comedy Festival** brings big names and new talent to venues throughout the city. Minimize the stress of the Thanksgiving holiday by gathering your chosen family for a Friendsgiving, or **letting Zabar's make your meal** while you curl up by the TV (or, if you're extremely lucky, your office window) to take in the **Macy's Thanksgiving Day Parade**.

OUTLOOK: *Marathon runners will appreciate clearing and chillier weather on the first of the month. In fact, all the way through Veterans Day, tranquil conditions prevail. Praise these days of warmth and haze, enjoy the calm while it lasts—for it's soon followed by wintry blasts. Some snow in the mountains, raining coastally; cold mostally. Gusty winds might play havoc with the Macy's balloons. Just say a blessing and pass the dressing!*

NORMALS FOR
CENTRAL PARK
Average High: 54.0°
Average Low: 42.0°
Average Liquid
Precipitation: 3.58"
Average Snowfall: 0.5"

Until 1939, Thanksgiving was always celebrated on the final Thursday of November. President Franklin Roosevelt then moved the holiday to the penultimate Thursday, but after backlash, signed a 1941 joint congressional resolution to celebrate it on the fourth Thursday. In NYC, the warmest Thanksgiving (69°) was Nov. 30, 1933. The coldest (15°) was Nov. 30, 1871. The rainiest (1.72") was Nov. 23, 2006, and the snowiest (4.4") was Nov. 23, 1989.

Sky Watch: If you have a clear view toward the east-southeast, look low to the horizon on November 7, about an hour before sunrise, to see a narrow crescent Moon passing just below brilliant Venus—and also, nearby, the bluish star Spica in Virgo. Binoculars will help. Saturn sits below the Moon on the 20th. Orion and the brilliant winter stars return this month, rising well before midnight.

ANNALS OF THE NIGHT SKY

Central Park is not a place one is likely to visit at midnight, but on November 17, 1966, the Hayden Planetarium, in cooperation with the Department of Parks, invited the public to Sheep Meadow to observe the Leonid meteor shower. In spite of cloudy skies, 10,000 persons assembled, listening attentively as astronomer Dr. Thomas D. Nicholson gave a forty-five-minute talk on astronomy. "The first rule in watching meteor showers," he told them cheerfully over a public address system, "is to pick a clear night." Half of the crowd booed, while the other half laughed.

NYC BOOK OF THE MONTH
This Beautiful, Ridiculous City: A Graphic Memoir
by Kay Sohini (2025)

A young woman's deep love for the literary city of Kerouac, Plath, and Bechdel develops into a passion for the real place in this memoir of an immigrant from India building and rebuilding a life in New York—while creating a city of her own through her vivid illustrations.

NYC MOVIE OF THE MONTH
The Landlord, directed by Hal Ashby, starring Beau Bridges, Lee Grant, Diana Sands, and Pearl Bailey (1970)

This prescient film about race and gentrification centers on Elgar Enders, a wealthy white Long Islander who buys a tenement building in Park Slope, Brooklyn. The exteriors were shot at 51 Prospect Place, near Sixth Avenue. Described in the film as "a dreadful slum," the block is home to brownstones that easily go for $3 million today.

Nov. 2–8

"New York is stirring, insupportable, agitated, ungovernable, demonic.... Not even Walt Whitman could today embrace it emotionally; the attempt might capsize him."
—Saul Bellow

2 MONDAY
☼ 6:27 AM / 4:51 PM

1993: 65 percent of Staten Islanders vote to secede from New York City in a non-binding referendum

3 TUESDAY
☼ 6:28 AM / 4:49 PM

Election Day

The Art Show at the Park Avenue Armory (through Nov. 7)

4 WEDNESDAY
☼ 6:29 AM / 4:48 PM

1955: Ticker tape parade for Carlos Castillo Armas, president of Guatemala

5 THURSDAY
☼ 6:31 AM / 4:47 PM

1941: Art Garfunkel is born in Forest Hills, Queens

6 FRIDAY
☼ 6:32 AM / 4:46 PM

Brooklyn Folk Festival (through Nov. 8)

7 SATURDAY
☼ 6:33 AM / 4:45 PM

1929: Museum of Modern Art opens

8 SUNDAY
☼ 6:34 AM / 4:44 PM

Diwali/Deepavali

Brooklyn Children's Book Fair at the Brooklyn Museum

Nov. 9–15

"The shapelessness and emptiness of the word *anywhere* appalls me as it appalls so many New Yorkers. So, very foolishly, we go on living in the only place in the universe which isn't just anywhere."
—Kurt Vonnegut

9 MONDAY

☼ 6:35 AM / 4:43 PM ● NEW MOON

1853: Architect Stanford White is born in New York

10 TUESDAY

☼ 6:37 AM / 4:42 PM

1939: Avant-garde jazz drummer Andrew Cyrille is born in Brooklyn

11 WEDNESDAY

☼ 6:38 AM / 4:41 PM

Veterans Day

Annual Veterans' Day Ceremony at the Intrepid Museum

12 THURSDAY

☼ 6:39 AM / 4:40 PM

Salon Art + Design at the Park Avenue Armory

13 FRIDAY

☼ 6:40 AM / 4:39 PM

1951: Ticker tape parade for the women of the armed forces

14 SATURDAY

☼ 6:41 AM / 4:38 PM

1907: New Yorker cartoonist and children's book author William Steig is born in Brooklyn

15 SUNDAY

☼ 6:42 AM / 4:37 PM

1968: Ol' Dirty Bastard (Russell Jones) is born in Brooklyn

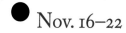

Nov. 16–22

"No matter how clever he may consider himself, no respectable man is a match for the villains and sharpers of New York."
—James D. McCabe, 1872

16 MONDAY

☼ 6:44 AM / 4:37 PM

1776: The Revolutionary War Battle of Fort Washington marks the end of Washington's disastrous New York campaign

17 TUESDAY

☼ 6:45 AM / 4:36 PM ☽ 1ST QUARTER

1920: Harlem's Apollo Theater opens

18 WEDNESDAY

☼ 6:46 AM / 4:35 PM

1919: Ticker tape parade for Edward Albert, Prince of Wales

19 THURSDAY

☼ 6:47 AM / 4:34 PM

1933: Larry King is born in New York City

20 FRIDAY

☼ 6:48 AM / 4:33 PM

Kweendom, a lineup of LGBTQ+ performers, at Pete's Candy Store (third Fridays)

21 SATURDAY

☼ 6:49 AM / 4:33 PM

1964: Verrazzano-Narrows Bridge opens

22 SUNDAY

☼ 6:51 AM / 4:33 PM ♐ SAGITTARIUS

1912: Heiress and philanthropist Doris Duke is born in New York City

Nov. 23–29

"It is the ambition of the New Yorker to live upon Fifth Avenue, to take his airings in the Park, and to sleep with his fathers in Green-Wood."
—*New York Times*, 1866

---

23 MONDAY
☼ 6:52 AM / 4:32 PM

1859 (or Sep. 17): Gunslinger Billy the Kid (Henry McCarty, a.k.a. William H. Bonney) is born in New York City

---

24 TUESDAY
☼ 6:53 AM / 4:31 PM   ○ FULL MOON

A Christmas Carol at the Merchant's House: Charles Dickens in New York, 1867 in the Merchant's House Museum's double parlor (through Dec. 27)

---

25 WEDNESDAY
☼ 6:54 AM / 4:31 PM

1783: Evacuation Day (when the last British troops left New York City)

---

26 THURSDAY
☼ 6:55 AM / 4:31 PM

Thanksgiving Day
Macy's Thanksgiving Day Parade

---

27 FRIDAY
☼ 6:56 AM / 4:30 PM

Native American Heritage Day

1746: Founding father Robert R. Livingston is born in New York City

---

28 SATURDAY
☼ 6:57 AM / 4:30 PM

1957: Radio City Rockettes make their first appearance at the Macy's Thanksgiving Day Parade

---

29 SUNDAY
☼ 6:58 AM / 4:29 PM

1991: ACT UP activists dressed as Santa Claus chain themselves inside Macy's to protest the exclusion of an HIV-positive Santa, Mark Woodley

DECEMBER

IN THE BRONX, a botanical city emerges in the **Haupt Conservatory of the New York Botanical Garden**. A half mile of railroad tracks weaves around almost 200 of the city's most iconic structures, from the Woolworth Building to the George Washington Bridge—all magically constructed not of steel, cast iron, or glass, but of leaves, acorns, and tree bark. Uptown at the Museum of the City of New York, a gingerbread and candy city pops up for *Gingerbread NYC: The Great Borough Bake-Off*. Restaurants like Rolf's, Lillie's Victorian, Pete's Tavern, and Oscar Wilde festoon themselves with holiday décor; even the most pedestrian Irish pubs throw up a few lights, garlands, and red-and-green ornaments. *Whimsy* is the word you're looking for. If you're really feeling it, or have a child or tourist in tow, the **Rockefeller Center Christmas Spectacular** or *The Nutcracker* at the New York City Ballet might just be your ticket to getting in the holiday spirit.

OUTLOOK: *The month starts with showers seeping, but by the 7th the snow is heaping; in the days that follow, pile on the blankets for good sleeping. Showers of snow and freezing rain glaze the glowing windowpane. Frostings of snow make angels glow. Christmastime is frigidly cold; freezing greetings! As the year comes to a close, skies turn fair and temps moderate. It's clear as a bell: to 2026 we bid farewell!*

NORMALS FOR
CENTRAL PARK
Average High: 44.3°
Average Low: 33.8°
Average Liquid
Precipitation: 4.38"
Average Snowfall: 4.9"

Sixty years ago, a Christmas Eve snowstorm swept across a wide area extending from the southern Plains states to New England. An intriguing aspect was the numerous reports of thunderstorms accompanied by heavy snow; hence this is known in some weather annals as the "Donner & Blitzen" storm. Central Park received 7.1" of snow, while most northern and western suburbs saw 10" to 12".

SKY WATCH: Beginning about 10 p.m. on the 13th and continuing through the rest of the night, we'll have a clear view of the Geminid meteor shower. It'll be at its very best between midnight and 4 a.m., when meteors will spray from Gemini, above Orion, at rates of up to one per minute. On the 23rd, the Moon will be 221,612 miles from Earth, making it an extra-big, extra-bright "supermoon."

ANNALS OF THE NIGHT SKY

Orbiting around the brightest star in the sky—the "Dog Star," Sirius, in Canis Major (the Big Dog)—is a white dwarf star known as the "Pup." Although probably no bigger than the Earth, the Pup is exceedingly dense. On our planet, a teaspoon of its material would weigh more than five tons! Currently, Sirius rises in the east-southeast around 8 p.m., crosses the meridian soon after midnight, and sets in the west-southwest at the break of dawn. The Pup can only be glimpsed with a moderately large telescope.

NYC BOOK OF THE MONTH
Sunshine: A Story about the City of New York by Ludwig Bemelmans (1950)

This one's a must-have for its cover alone: a comic scene of the lower Manhattan skyline during a downpour, complete with the Statue of Liberty holding aloft an umbrella. Bemelmans illustrates a city that is (as Adam Gopnik wrote in a review) "cop-on-the-beat blue and brownstone brown" for this children's story of a music teacher and a noise complaint.

NYC MOVIE OF THE MONTH
Smoke, directed by Wayne Wang, starring William Hurt, Harvey Keitel, Stockard Channing, and others (1995)

Scriptwriter Paul Auster brings his Park Slope neighborhood to life in a tale that shows the other side of the gentrification in *The Landlord*. The protagonist is Paul, a writer with writer's block, but the heart of the film is Harvey Keitel's Auggie, who has photographed the street outside his cigar store at 8 a.m. every day for decades. Auggie gives Paul a Christmas story about how he got his camera, an anecdote that lyrically reflects the neighborhood's complexity.

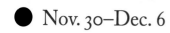

Nov. 30–Dec. 6

"New York is a realm of fantasy and myth, obsession and resentment, fear and bewilderment for many who've never set foot in it."
—Richard Brody

30 MONDAY
☼ 6:59 AM / 4:29 PM

Last chance to see Tatiana Arocha at the Sunset Park Library

1 TUESDAY
☼ 7:00 AM / 4:29 PM   ◐ 3RD QUARTER

1952: *Daily News* runs the headline "Ex-GI Becomes Blonde Beauty," reporting on the first widely known successful gender reassignment surgery

2 WEDNESDAY
☼ 7:01 AM / 4:29 PM

Rockefeller Center Christmas Tree Lighting

3 THURSDAY
☼ 7:02 AM / 4:28 PM

1935: First Houses, NYC's first public housing, opens

4 FRIDAY
☼ 7:03 AM / 4:28 PM

1783: Nine days after the last British soldiers leave, General George Washington bids farewell to his officers at Fraunces Tavern

5 SATURDAY
☼ 7:04 AM / 4:28 PM

Hanukkah begins.

1967: Dr. Benjamin Spock and Allen Ginsberg are arrested along with 262 others while protesting the Vietnam War in New York City

6 SUNDAY
☼ 7:05 AM / 4:28 PM

1896: Ira Gershwin is born in New York City

Dec. 7–13

"Each generation is drawn by a collective memory of New York and the miracle of regeneration."
—Ada Louise Huxtable

7 MONDAY

☼ 7:06 AM / 4:28 PM

Pearl Harbor Remembrance Day

1842: New York Philharmonic's first concert

8 TUESDAY

☼ 7:07 AM / 4:28 PM

1925: Sammy Davis Jr. is born in Harlem

9 WEDNESDAY

☼ 7:08 AM / 4:28 PM ● NEW MOON

1955: Ticker tape parade for Luis Batlle Berres, president of Uruguay

10 THURSDAY

☼ 7:09 AM / 4:28 PM

1946: Actor Gloria Loring is born in New York City

11 FRIDAY

☼ 7:09 AM / 4:28 PM

1732: The Nassau Street Theatre, the city's first concert hall, opens

12 SATURDAY

☼ 7:10 AM / 4:28 PM

Hanukkah ends.

1848: William Kissam Vanderbilt is born in New Dorp, Staten Island

13 SUNDAY

☼ 7:11 AM / 4:29 PM

1957: Steve Buscemi is born in New York City

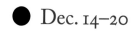

Dec. 14–20

"How do Americans think of New York?... It is our legendary phenomenon, our great thing, our world-famous impossibility. Some seem to wish that it were nothing more than a persistent rumor."
—Saul Bellow

14 MONDAY
☼ 7:12 AM / 4:29 PM

1945: Ticker tape parade for Fleet Admiral William F. Halsey Jr.

15 TUESDAY
☼ 7:12 AM / 4:29 PM

1936: Eddie Palmieri, father of salsa music, is born in Spanish Harlem

16 WEDNESDAY
☼ 7:13 AM / 4:29 PM ◐ 1ST QUARTER

1835: The Great Fire destroys nearly 700 buildings in Lower Manhattan

17 THURSDAY
☼ 7:14 AM / 4:30 PM

1980: Coca Crystal interviews Abbie Hoffman on her public access show *If I Can't Dance, You Can Keep Your Revolution*

18 FRIDAY
☼ 7:14 AM / 4:30 PM

1980: Christina Aguilera is born on Staten Island

19 SATURDAY
☼ 7:15 AM / 4:30 PM

1945: Dorothy Shaver is named president of Lord & Taylor, becoming the first female executive of a department store

20 SUNDAY
☼ 7:16 AM / 4:31 PM

1865: Decorator Elsie de Wolfe is born in New York City

Dec. 21–27

"Everybody writes about New York with so much tenderness, even when they are sick of it."
—Kay Sohini

21 MONDAY

☼ 7:16 AM / 4:31 PM ♑ CAPRICORN

Winter Solstice

1937: Jane Fonda is born in Manhattan

22 TUESDAY

☼ 7:17 AM / 4:32 PM

1799: Elma Sands disappears, leading to the Manhattan Well Murder trial, the first US murder trial with a transcript

23 WEDNESDAY

☼ 7:17 AM / 4:32 PM

Radio City Rockettes Christmas Spectacular (Nov. through Jan. 3, 2027)

24 THURSDAY

☼ 7:17 AM / 4:33 PM
○ FULL MOON

Christmas Eve

Last chance to visit the Union Square Holiday Market for last-minute gifts

25 FRIDAY

☼ 7:18 AM / 4:34 PM

Christmas Day

Eat at a Chinese restaurant

26 SATURDAY

☼ 7:18 AM / 4:34 PM

Kwanzaa begins.

1820: Dion Boucicault, who produced the anti-slavery play *The Octoroon* at Broadway's Winter Garden Theatre in 1859, is born in Dublin

27 SUNDAY

☼ 7:18 AM / 4:35 PM

1932: Radio City Music Hall opens

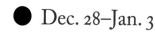
Dec. 28–Jan. 3

"Whoever said, 'Nothing good happens after midnight' has never lived in New York."
– Lena Dunham

28 MONDAY
☼ 7:19 AM / 4:36 PM

1953: Director James Foley is born in Brooklyn

29 TUESDAY
☼ 7:19 AM / 4:36 PM

1939: First college basketball doubleheader is played at Madison Square Garden

30 WEDNESDAY
☼ 7:19 AM / 4:37 PM   ◐ 1ST QUARTER

1873: Al Smith is born in the Fourth Ward on the Lower East Side

31 THURSDAY
☼ 7:19 AM / 4:38 PM

New Year's Eve
Times Square Ball Drop

1 FRIDAY
☼ 7:20 AM / 4:39 PM

New Year's Day
Kwanzaa ends.
Hide under the covers

2 SATURDAY
☼ 7:20 AM / 4:40 PM

1889: *Puck* magazine's cover pokes fun at the Metropolitan Museum of Art for being closed on Sundays, the average person's day off

3 SUNDAY
☼ 7:20 AM / 4:40 PM

1897: Actor Marion Davies is born in Brooklyn"

Contributors

GENERAL EDITOR **Susan Gail Johnson** is a museum consultant, editor, and content developer with a special expertise in New York City. She managed numerous major exhibitions and publications for the Museum of the City of New York and served as project director of its institution-defining permanent exhibition, *New York at Its Core*. Johnson holds a master's degree from NYU's John W. Draper Interdisciplinary Program in Humanities and Social Thought.

ASTRONOMER **Joe Rao** is an Associate and Guest Lecturer at the Hayden Planetarium of the American Museum of Natural History, astronomy columnist for *Natural History* magazine, Night Sky columnist for Space.com, and a contributing editor at *Sky and Telescope* magazine.

METEOROLOGIST **Professor Vaticinate** is the nom de plume of an experienced professional meteorologist.

FASHION FORECASTER **Raissa Bretaña** is a New York–based fashion historian and adjunct instructor at the Fashion Institute of Technology. She also hosts a popular video series for *Glamour*.

ILLUSTRATOR **Andrey Kokorin's** work has appeared in magazines, advertisements, and product packaging around the world.

Compilation copyright © 2025 Abbeville Press. All rights reserved under international copyright conventions. No part of this book may be reproduced or utilized in any form or by any means, electronic or mechanical, including photocopying, recording, or by any information retrieval system, without permission in writing from the publisher. Inquiries should be addressed to Abbeville Press, 655 Third Avenue, New York, NY 10017. The text of this book was set in Caslon Pro. Printed in Türkiye.

ISBN 978-0-7892-5477-1

Fifth edition
1 3 5 7 9 10 8 6 4 2

This almanac is published by Abbeville Press, www.abbeville.com.
For bulk and premium sales, call 1-800-ARTBOOK.
Customized covers and complimentary point-of-sale displays are
available with bulk orders of the almanac.